SLAVERY IN INDIA

SLAVERY IN INDIA.

THE PRESENT STATE

OF

EAST INDIA SLAVERY;

CHIEFLY EXTRACTED FROM THE

PARLIAMENTARY PAPERS ON THE SUBJECT.

BY JAMES PEGGS

GYAN

Published by

GYAN

Gyan Publishing House
5, Ansari Road
Daryaganj, New Delhi-110002
Phone: 011-47034999, 9811692060
E-mail: books@gyanbooks.com

Distribution Network
gyanbooks.com
India, USA, Canada, UK, Australia

ISBN: 978-93-6433-441-9 (PB)
First Published, 1840

2nd Impression 2024

Printed at: Gyan Press, Delhi.

SLAVERY IN INDIA
Author: JAMES PEGGS

SLAVERY IN INDIA.

THE PRESENT STATE

OF

EAST INDIA SLAVERY;

CHIEFLY EXTRACTED FROM THE

PARLIAMENTARY PAPERS ON THE SUBJECT.

Printed March, 1828, *Aug*. 1832. *Aug*. 1838.

By JAMES PEGGS,

LATE MISSIONARY IN ORISSA;

AUTHOR OF "INDIA'S CRIES TO BRITISH HUMANITY;" A PRIZE ESSAY ON "THE ABOLITION OF CAPITAL PUNISHMENT," &c.

THIRD EDITION, REVISED AND ENLARGED.

"Slavery in every form is an evil of great magnitude, and peculiarly revolting to the moral feelings of Englishmen."—*The Hon. Court of Directors.*

"The outcry raised in India against the *Suttee* was long powerless, until it returned reverberated from the British shores; and that against *Slavery* will continue disregarded, unless it receive support from all the energy of the Home Government."—*Par. Papers*, 1832.

LONDON:

PUBLISHED FOR THE AUTHOR,

BY G. WIGHTMAN, 24, PATERNOSTER ROW;

SOLD BY WAUGH AND INNES, EDINBURGH, AND KEENE, DUBLIN.

1840.

CONTENTS.

CHAPTER I.

CHAPTER II.

CHAPTER III.

CHAPTER IV.

EAST INDIA SLAVERY.

CHAP. I.

Introductory Remarks—Origin, Nature, and Evils of Slavery in India and the Eastern Islands.

A GREAT want of correct information respecting the nature and extent of East India slavery, is very prevalent in Great Britain, and also in many parts of India. The late Bishop Heber, in his interesting journal, has the following observation—" Though *no Slavery legally exists in the British territories at this moment*, yet the terms and gestures used by servants to their superiors, all imply that such a distinction was at no distant date very common. 'I am thy slave,' 'thy slave has no knowledge,' are continually used as expressions of submission and ignorance." Another writer upon India, whose work was published in that country, in 1823, falls into the same error. An extract or two may suffice: " Slavery is now entirely prohibited here (Bengal) by the British Government, as really as in Britain itself. In consequence of this, whatever of this nature exists at present, is conducted in secret, like all other acts of injustice, robbery, and iniquity. Nor is the act of selling a slave more fully covered by darkness, than the fact of holding persons in a state of slavery. No native dares openly avow that he holds a fellow-creature in slavery; although from the concealment which, enveloping the economy of native families, hides them so fully from European view, it may probably be the case, while forbidden by the British laws, and held in such abhorrence by British functionaries of justice. It is some little consolation to learn, that in India there can be no *hereditary* slavery, and that the children of persons unhappily sold into slavery, of themselves go out free. It is only the person actually sold who is in bondage; over their children, according to the natives themselves, their owners have no right whatever. Thus, the worst features in West Indian slavery is not found at all in that which has hitherto obtained in India."* That such erroneous statements, upon this subject, should be published by residents in India, is very much to be regretted; but it arises from the prevalence of slavery in those parts of the country, with which the writers were not acquainted. The same want of information is observable in some public men who have returned from India, and expressed their opinions. On the renewal of the East India Charter, in 1833, it was proposed by the King's ministers to abolish slavery in British India, on or before April 12, 1837, but this was overruled in the House of Lords; on which occasion the Duke of Wellington said, "I insist upon it that there exists no necessity for framing any laws or regulations with regard to slavery in the East Indies. I have served in that country, and lived among the people, and I never knew an instance of cruelty being practised towards the slaves, if slaves they ought to be called!" At a recent meeting of the British and Foreign Anti-Slavery Society in London, one of the speakers, who has paid very great attention to the slavery subject declared,—"Slavery has been so nearly extinguished in the British dominions, that if it were found *lurking in any remote corner of the empire*, and could be fully exposed, he believed the nation was prepared to crush it at once and for ever! He trusted that they had arrived at the happy period when slavery can no longer be considered as one of their national crimes; and that therefore they might consistently unite with the anti-slavery friends in other parts of the world, labouring for the attainment of the same great object."

The error of this estimable friend (in common with that of many others), arose from not duly considering the extent of the great measure for the abolition of colonial, or rather of negro slavery. British India and the Eastern Isles were unhappily excluded from the range of that noble effort of Christian philanthropy. The clause in the new Indian Charter, passed August, 1833, relative to East India Slavery is as follows;—"And be it further enacted, that the said Govern-

* Friend of India (Quar. Ser.), Dec. 1823. The Patriot, July 17, 1833.

or-general in council shall, and he is hereby required forthwith to take into consideration the means of mitigating the state of slavery, and of ameliorating the condition of slaves, and of extinguishing slavery throughout the said territories, so soon as such extinction shall be practicable and safe; and from time to time to prepare and transmit to the said Court of Directors, drafts of laws and regulations for the purposes aforesaid; and that in preparing such drafts, due regard shall be had to the laws of marriage, and the rights and authorities of fathers and heads of families; and that such drafts shall forthwith after receipt thereof be taken into consideration by the said Court of Directors, who shall with all convenient speed communicate to the said Governor-general in council their instructions on the drafts of the said laws and regulations but no such laws and regulations shall be promulgated or put into force without the previous consent of the said court; and the said court shall within fourteen days after the first meeting of parliament in every year, lay before both houses of parliament a report of the drafts of such rules and regulations as shall have been received by them, and of their resolutions thereon." We have seen the date of this act, and may naturally ask, what has been done for the Indian slave "to break his yoke and let him go free?" On Aug. 7, 1839, in reply to a question from Mr. Ewart, to Sir J. C. Hobhouse, President of the India Board, it was stated—"That there is a Commission sitting in India upon the subject of slavery, and that as soon as its labours should be concluded, a report would be forwarded to this country." From these tardy proceedings it may be justly feared that many years will elapse before East India slavery will be abolished.

It is very much to be regretted that while so much has been written upon negro slavery, so little exists upon East India slavery.* The voluminous Parliamentary Papers of March 1828, August 1832, and July 1838, from their voluminousness, afford but little specific information; and it has been remarked, "an attempt to digest such a mass of documents into a narrative, or to reduce them into any symmetrical shape is hopeless." The author has not been thus discouraged in his investigation of them; but being convinced that slavery in India is a subject of very great interest, he has devoted much time to the study of these papers, and hopes

* See East and West India Sugar, 1823. Hatchard. East India Slavery, by Saintsbury. 1829.

that his labours may be beneficial to the interests of humanity and of our common christianity in the East. To bring the real state of India before the British people, appears highly desirable, and under this conviction the author submits his humble labours to the candid attention of his readers.

J. Richardson, Esq., Judge and Magistrate of *Bundlecund*, in his valuable communication to the British Government in India, on the subject of slavery, in 1808, very justly remarks, —"The humane abolition of the slave-trade in England, has added lustre to the enlightened wisdom of the British senate; and enrolled, to the latest posterity, the name of Wilberforce amongst the benefactors of mankind. That slavery should ever have been authorized, in any civilized community, is as astonishing to the mind, as disgraceful to human nature. The great Author of creation made all men equally free. By what act then can that freedom be forfeited or given up? Surely liberty can be forfeited by no act that does not militate against the general security and well-being of society. Nor has man more right to sell or give up the natural freedom of his person, than he has to lay down his natural life at pleasure; much less can he have any title to dispose of the liberty of another, even of his child. That *slavery is an infringement of the law of nature cannot be disputed*. The most respectable authority proves that it is in its own nature invalid. Blackstone, speaking of the law of nature, says, 'this law of nature, coeval with mankind, and dictated by God himself, is superior in obligation to any other. It is binding all over the globe, in all countries, and at all times; no human laws are of any validity if contrary to this; and such of them as are valid, derive all their force and authority mediately and immediately from this original.' The most strenuous defenders of this imposition of the powerful over the weaker part of mankind, pretend not to maintain its propriety but on ideas of political utility. Impartial and minute inquiry into its effects would at once remove this specious veil, by which the principle is sometimes hidden, and the system, decorated in the eye of sensible and virtuous men under mistaken notions of human expediency, proves the uniform tendency of slavery to be depressive of every emanation of the mind, and highly destructive to our species."*

The origin of slavery in India, as it exists among the

* Par. Papers on Slavery in India, 1828, p. 299. There is much truth in the observation,—"He who loses his liberty, loses half his virtue."

Hindoos, is involved in considerable obscurity. "Of agrestic or prædial slavery," says T. H. Baber, Esq., "the origin is of very remote antiquity. The general term for this description of slavery is *adami*, or literally as I understand the term, *serf, aboriginal*, or *indigenous*, being held precisely under the same tenure as the land itself throughout (under some slight modifications) the *Malabar* coast, in the *Balagant* districts, and even in the western parts of the table land of *Mysore*."* Its rise among the Mussulman is evidently to be traced to the triumph of their arms. The following extracts from the voluminous Parliamentary Papers on slavery in India, afford much information upon a subject interesting to every humane mind. These Papers commence with a Regulation for punishing decoits or robbers, and show one source of slavery in the East.—"That whereas the peace of this country hath for some years past been greatly disturbed by bands of decoits, who not only infest the high roads, but often plunder whole villages, burning the houses, and murdering the inhabitants: And whereas these abandoned outlaws have hitherto found means to elude every attempt which the vigilance of government hath put in force, for detecting and bringing such atrocious criminals to justice, by the secresy of their haunts, and the wild state of the districts which are most subject to their incursions; it becomes the indispensable duty of government to try the most rigorous means, since experience has proved every lenient and ordinary remedy to be ineffectual. That it be therefore resolved, That every such criminal, on conviction, shall be carried to the village to which he belongs, and be there executed for a terror and example to others; and, for the further prevention of such abominable practices, that the village, of which he is an inhabitant, shall be fined according to the enormity of the crime, and each inhabitant according to his substance; and that, *the family of the criminal shall become the slaves of the State, and be disposed of for the general benefit and convenience of the people, according to the discretion of the government*. Aug. 1772."†

"If we may judge (says the Editor of the Asiatic Journal, in a review of the contents of these Papers) from a subsequent minute and regulation of the Bengal Government (1774), this proposal was not listened to; for therein, not only is the stealing of children or selling any Hindoo as a slave (without

* Par. Papers, 1832, p. 551.

† Par. Papers, p. 2.

a regular deed) forbidden, but it is proposed to abolish slavery altogether, after the first generation then living, owing to *the great increase of late years of this savage commerce, and in order to prevent hasty strides towards depopulation.* Further inquiry, however, seems to have convinced the Bengal Government, that there were *districts where slavery was in general usage*, and the abolition of which might impede cultivation. The Government observes, that the opinions of the most creditable Mussulman and Hindoo inhabitants condemn the usage of selling slaves, as repugnant to the particular precepts both of the Koran and the Shaster."*

The Provincial Council of *Patna*, in Aug. 1774, address the Governor, Warren Hastings, Esq., on this subject, as follows:—"We find that there are two kinds of slaves in this province, Mussulman and Hindoo; the former are properly called Mualazadeh, and the latter Kahaar. *Slaves of either denomination are considered in the same light as any other property, and are transferable by the owner, or descend at his demise to his heirs.* They date the rise of the custom of Kahaar slavery from the first incursions of the Mahomedans, when the captives were distributed by the general among the officers of his army, to whose posterity they remained. All other slaves have become so by occasional purchase, as in cases of famine, &c. The Kaboleh must be signed by the mother or grandmother, and not by the father. Children also born of slaves are *the property of the owner of the woman*, though married to a slave of a different family."†

The Collector of *Trichinopoly*, in the Madras Presidency, in reply to the inquiries of the Government, addressed to a number of Collectors on the subject of slavery in their respective districts, thus describes the origin of the *pullers*, or agricultural slavery.—"It is, I apprehend, indisputable, that in the earliest ages of Hindoo government, agricultural and domestic slavery existed to an indefinite extent. The practice was sanctioned by prescription and upheld by law; but it will be found that the terms of bondage, and the nature of the services required from the slaves, differed essentially in almost every district. No distinct information can be obtained at what period agricultural slavery commenced. It is now impossible to trace, whether this establishment took it rise from the voluntary submission of the indigent to the wealthy, or whether the pullers were originally captives taken in war. But, as this species of bondage is generally the concomitant

* Asi. Journ. Nov. 1828, p. 559. † Par. Papers, on Slavery in India, p. 5.

of barbarous governments, it must of necessity have been a very ancient institution of the Hindoos. Under their arbitrary government, the distinctions of caste were scrupulously maintained; and, adverting to the circumstance of the meerassidars in Trichinopoly being Brahmuns, it scarcely excites surprise that *agricultural slavery should exist here unchanged and undiminished.*"*

"It cannot escape observation," says the Chief Judge Leycester, in 1823, "that the extension of our territory *has greatly added to the increase of this detestable traffic* (in slaves), and its far more detestable impunity. British protection has had the peculiar property of branding nations with slavery, who, as far as we were concerned, were protected from it before; that *under the show of British liberality and justice lurked the envenomed taint*—that successively as the ceded provinces were transferred to us, as Nepaul was conquered and the Mahratta combination annihilated, each act of sovereignty carried with it a secret clause, 'You may now, your wives and children, be removed into Bengal, as slaves; and at the caprice of a slave-master, a man's wife being what is termed a slave, may, with his children by her, be carried off from him to any remote corner of the province, boasting the enjoyment of British protection'!"†

The late Sir Stamford Raffles, Lieut. Governor of *the Island of Java,* in 1812, gives the following information, respecting the origin of slavery in the Eastern Isles:—

"*Macassar* and its neighbourhood may be considered as a principal source from which slaves have been exported; and without entering into any discussion of the origin and causes of this state of society, which, in a general point of view, must be referred to *backwardness of civilization and prevalence of native authority,* it must be observed that, in consequence of its being the favourite source of revenue among those chieftains, it will require much caution in attempting any measures to restrain, where argument could be of no avail, and force would be inconvenient. In my instructions to Captain Phillips, on his proceeding to Macassar, I directed his attention in a particular manner to this interesting subject; but I regret to find from his report, that at present there is little prospect of his favourable interference. In short, he seems decidedly of opinion that, 'as men-stealers are very common over the country, if he prohibited their selling their stolen property at Macassar, they would still carry on the trade in the Boui territory;' where, though so immediately under the eye of the Resident, the Rajah would no doubt maintain his right, equally with that which he exercises at pleasure, of life and death.

"The native laws, usages, and habits, regarding slavery, are in many instances so various and contradictory, and it is so difficult to trace them to any authentic source that is universally admitted, that I am fearful very little light will be obtained from them. Prisoners of war are in many cases considered as the property of the conqueror, and consequently sold as slaves. The families of

* Par. Papers, p, 892. † Ib. 1838, p. 315.

criminals, who may be executed for particular crimes, become likewise a droit of the chief; and in many cases criminals are pardoned on condition of being sold into slavery. Throughout the whole of the Eastern Islands, debtors become responsible in their services to their creditors; and it does not appear that there is any generally acknowledged law among them, to prevent the chief of a family selling his wife and children into slavery. The desperate manner in which the Bugguese prows are known to defend themselves at sea, is accounted for by the numerous crew, who are all *separate adventurers on a borrowed capital*, having left their families hypothecated for the debt, who become slaves to the creditor in the event of the debtor parting with the property under any circumstances without his life.

"The Dutch law being blended with the Roman, and the colonial law founded on both, slavery has been fully recognised as legal by the European government; while the universal prevalence of Mahomedanism renders it legal with every native administration; and as such it appears, without any occasional difference of opinion, to have been always viewed. Slavery on the island of Java, is exclusively confined to domestic purposes, and may be considered rather as a regulated domestic servitude, than that detestable system which the legislature of Great Britain have, to the credit of humanity, so vigorously suppressed in the West Indies. *Slavery, however, under any shape, or if it bears only the name, is so repugnant to every principle of enlightened administration, and so inconsistent with your Lordship's* benevolent plans, that I fear I should not stand excused, in my defence of such a system, under any modifications or circumstances whatever.*"†

The rise of slavery in *Penang*, or *Prince of Wales' Island*, is thus described in a letter from the Judge in 1802, to the Marquis of Wellesley, then Governor General of India:—

"My Lord Marquis:—In a case which lately came judicially before me, a question arose, '*Whether civil slavery, that is, a right of one man over the person and fortune of another, was to be considered as established at Prince of Wales' Island.*' I was not ignorant that slavery, limited and unlimited, had been tolerated. I know that emigrants from the Malay Peninsula, and from the Eastern Island, who had become inhabitants of Prince of Wales' Island, have been permitted to retain in slavery, those whom they had brought as slaves to this place. Some of these, indeed, are in entire slavery, while others are only in limited servitude. The latter is the condition of those who are styled slave debtors, and these are people that voluntarily become slaves to their creditors till their debts are paid. But all this passed *sub silentio*; for, after a careful search, I have not found any regulation of the local government, or any order from the Governor General in council, authorizing the establishment of slavery, limited or unlimited, at Prince of Wales' Island. This right, if any such in fact exists, rests therefore *simply on a usage of fourteen years*. Thus circumstanced, having no authority to guide my judgment, my delicacy increased in proportion to the interests on which I was called to determine; and, in this case, subordinate to the question of civil slavery, arose two other questions. The first a question of fact, 'Whether the father of A. ever had been a slave at Quiddah?' The second a question of law, 'What was to be the condition of A. now resident at Prince of Wales' Island, whether born of one parent who was free, and of another who was enslaved, or born of parents who were both slaves, and now resident at Prince of Wales' Island?'

"I was desirous of avoiding the determination of this case, and remitted it to the Lieutenant Governor; but, in deference to his particular request, I gave

* Lord Minto. † Par. Papers, p. 154—156. For an account of the slave-trade at the island of *Nias*, near *Sumatra*, see an interesting article from the *Singapore Chronicle*, in the *Imperial Mag. Jan.* 1830, pp. 48—54.

my opinion, that *the evidence did not prove that the father ever had been a slave, but that it inclined to show that the mother had been a slave at Quiddah, and I thought the son should follow the condition of his father.* I was led to this opinion, from a consideration that it is the old law of villanage in England, and, although I knew it was contrary to the maxim of the civilians, *partes sequitur ventrem*, yet the latter authority had no weight with me; first, because slavery had not yet been established by authority; next, because I could not see any local circumstance requiring its establishment; and lastly, because *a state of slavery, is in its own nature, bad, neither useful to the master nor to the slave, nor to the state under which they live.* The Lieutenant Governor, on the contrary, was of opinion that the evidence proved both parents of A. were slaves, and under the regulations for the administration of justice on this island, ultimately decreed, that A., resident in this island, should be delivered up as a slave to Hakim Sullee, Captain Malay, resident also on this island.

"By this decree slavery is now recognized by the local government of this island; and therefore, in addition to the observations which I have had the honour of submitting to the consideration of your Excellency in council, I feel the necessity of representing that regulations are now requisite, in which the right that a master is to possess over the person and fortune of his slave, at Prince of Wales' Island, should be explicitly defined; and I hope that your Excellency in council will take into consideration *the case of the offspring of slaves*, and particularly of those, who are born of one parent who is free, while the other is a slave. Nothing can be presumed on the moderation or justice of Mahomedans who possess slaves. By their usages the virtue or honour of female slaves is at the mercy of their master! I could hope that the right of the master was by law expressly limited to the bounds of humanity. I have no other apology to offer, than my conviction, that the subject matter of my letter is of the first importance to the interests and prosperity of this rising colony."*

"The countries," says E. Presgrave, Esq., Acting Resident Council for *Malacca*, "which supply the slaves or slave debtors (for they are one), are the *Battas*, the *Balli*, the interior of *Borneo*, called *Daya Ro*, and a few from the island of *Nias*. One of the most fertile sources of supply of slaves undoubtedly is piracy; to this end chiefly are these piratical expeditions directed, and the profits arising from the sale of the captives, is at once the inducement and main support of these barbarous and destructive undertakings. Many are imported directly from the above places by native traders; many are *hereditary* slaves, persons condemned to slavery by the native laws, or taken in war, or kidnapped by the traders."†

The nature of slavery in India will appear from the following extracts. The Governor General, in 1775, transmitted to the Hon. Court of Directors, extracts from a translation of the Hindoo Laws, by N. B. Halhed, Esq. From this code, it appears that slaves are divided into *fifteen* classes, viz.—

"1. Whoever is born of a female slave, and is called Gerbejat.
2. Whoever is purchased for a price, and is called Keereeut.

* Par. Papers on Slavery in India, 1828, pp. 429, 430.
† Par. Papers, 1838, p. 306.

3. Whoever is found *anywhere by chance*, and is called Lubdehee.

4. Whoever is a slave by descent from his ancestors, and is called Dayavaupakut.

5. Whoever hath been fed, and hath had his life preserved by another during a famine, and is called Enakal Behrut.

6. Whoever hath been delivered up as a pledge for money borrowed, and is called Abut.

7. Whoever, to free himself from the debt of a creditor, hath borrowed money from another person, and, having discharged the old debt, gives himself up as a servant to the person with whom the present debt is contracted; or whoever, by way of terminating the importunities of a creditor, delivers himself up for a servant to that creditor, and is called Mookhud.

8. Whoever hath been enslaved by the fortune of battle, and is called Joodih Peeraput.

9. Whoever becomes a slave by a loss on the chances of dice, or other games, and is called Punjeet; according to the ordinations of Perkashkar and Pareejaut, and according to the ordination of Chendeesur, it is thus, that by whatever chance he is conquered, and becomes a slave, he is called Punjeet—approved.

10. Whoever of his own desire says to another, "I am become your slave," and is called Opookut.

11. When a Chebteree, or Bice, having become Sinassee (religious mendicants) apostates from that way of life, the magistrate shall make him a slave, and is called Perberjabesheet.

12. Whoever voluntarily gives himself as a slave to another for a stipulated time, and is called Gheerut.

13. Whoever performs servitude for his subsistence, and is called Bheekut.

14. Whoever, from the desire of possessing a slave girl, becomes a slave, and is called Berbakrut.

15. Whoever of his own accord sells his liberty, and becomes a slave, and is called Bekreet."*

Sir R. Chambers, on the trial of the commander of a Danish trading vessel, for procuring native children, and exporting them as slaves, in 1789, stated *the only cases in which slavery was lawful under the Mussulman Government*.—"Infidels, taken prisoners in war, fighting against Mussulmans, were considered the slaves of the captors; and the slavery extended to their children. In cases of famine, publicly declared, it was lawful for farmers to sell their children; and persons of more than *fifteen years of age*, might sell themselves to obtain a subsistence. But that in these *four cases only*, the condition of slavery was put under many legal restrictions, and that it was *unlawful for a Mussulman to sell his slave*. That the exportation of subjects of a Mussulman government to be sold to a state of slavery was unknown; and, he believed, that it was the first time such an offence had been committed under the British flag, and he trusted it would be the last. He wished it to be understood that, if a similar offence should ever unhappily be again tried before the court, the punishment would be more severe."†

* Par. Papers. pp. 7, 300.

† Par. Papers on Slavery in India, 1828, p. 21.

The nature of slavery, Hindoo and Mussulman, will appear by the following extract, from the valuable communications to the Bengal Government, of the Magistrate of *Bundlecund.* This gentleman observes,—" Previously to my submission of the draught of the regulation directed to be submitted to the court of Nizamut Adawlut, I deem it of essential importance to the elucidation of the subject, to offer a few remarks, *on the laws of slavery as they now exist in that part of Hindostan,* which it has pleased God to allot to the government of the British nation. For the sake of perspicuity, I shall transcribe the questions put to the Mahomedan and Hindoo law officers officially, for the purpose of procuring *a declaration of law on the subject of slavery,* according to their respective codes,—insert their answers, and,—offer such remarks as present themselves to my judgment, or as seem applicable to the subject.

Questions put to the Muftee by the Nizamut Adawlut.

First Ques. " *What description of slaves are authorized by the Mahomedan law?*"

Ans. " All men are by nature free and independent, and *no man can be a subject of property, except an infidel inhabiting a country not under the power and control of the faithful.* This right of possession which the Moslems have over Hurbus (infidels fighting against the faith), is acquired by *Isteela,* which means, *the entire subdument of any subject of property by force of arms.* The original right of property, which one man may possess over another, is to be acquired *solely by Isteela,* and cannot be obtained in the first instance by purchase, donation, or heritage. When, therefore, an Imaum subdues, by force of arms, any one of the cities inhabited by infidels, such of them as may be taken prisoners become his rightful property, and he has the power of putting them to death or making them slaves, and distributing them as such among the ghazees (victorious soldiers), particularly when fighting against infidels; or he may set them at liberty in a Mussulman country, and levy the capitation tax; should he make them slaves, they become legal subjects of property, and are transferable by sale, gift, or inheritance. But if, after captivity, *they should become converts to Islam* (the faith) *the power of death over them is thereby barred, though they would continue slaves;* for, slavery being the necessary consequence of original infidelity, the conversion to Islam does not affect the prior state of bondage to which the individual has been regularly rendered liable by Isteela, provided this be clearly established. From this it is evident that the same rules are applicable to the slaves of both sexes. If slaves are afterwards sold, or given away, by the Imaum, or by the ghazees, who shared at the distribution, or if they should become the property of another by inheritance, they then become slaves under the three different classes of purchase, donation, and inheritance.

"If a female should bear offspring, by any other than by her legal lord and master, whether the father be a freeman or a slave, and whether the slave of the said master, or of any other person, in any one of these cases, such offspring is subject to slavery, and these are called *khanazad* (born in the family); but, if the children be the acknowledged offspring of the right owner, *they are then free*, and *the mother of them* (being the parent of a child by her master) *becomes, at his decease, free also; and this rule is applicable to all their descendants to the latest posterity.* The practice among free men and women of selling their own offspring, during the time of famine, is exceedingly improper and unjustifiable, being in direct opposition to the principle above stated, viz. *that no man can be a subject of property, except an infidel taken in the act of hostilities against the faith.* In no case can a person, legally free, become a subject of property; and *children not being the property of their parents, all sales or purchases of them, as any other articles of illegal property, are consequently invalid.* It is also illegal for any free man to sell his own person, either in time of famine or though he be oppressed by a debt which he is unable to discharge. For in the first of these cases a famished man may feed upon a dead body ! or may rob another ; and a distressed debtor is not liable to any fine or punishment.

"We are not acquainted with the principal or detailed circumstances, which led to the custom prevailing in most Mussulman countries of purchasing and selling the inhabitants of *Zanguibar*, *Ethiopia*, *Nubia*, and other *Negros :* but the ostensible causes are, either that the negros sell their own offspring, or that Mussulman or other tribes of people take them prisoners by fraud, or seize them by stealth from the sea shores. In such cases, *they are not legally slaves, and the sale and purchase of them are consequently invalid.* But if a Mussulman army, by order of an Imaum, should invade their country, and make them prisoners of war by force of arms, they are then legal slaves ; provided that such negros are inhabitants of a country under the government of Infidels, and in which a Mussulman is not entitled to receive the full benefit and protection of his own laws. With regard to the custom, prevailing in this country, of hiring children from their parents, for a very considerable period, such as for seventy or eighty years, and under this pretext making them slaves, as well as their produce also, under the denomination of *kharazad* (domestic slaves), the following laws are applicable;—*It is lawful and proper for parents to hire out their children on service, but this contract of hire becomes null and void when the child arrives at the years of discretion; as the right of parentage then ceases.* A free man, who has reached the years of discretion, may enter into a contract to serve another, but not for any great length of time such as for seventy years; as this also is a mere pretext, and has the same object of slavery in view, whereas the said free man has the option of dissolving any contract of hire under either of the following circumstances:—It is the custom, in *contracts* of this nature, for a person hired on service to receive a compensation in money, clothes, and food, as the price of hire; any day therefore that a servant receives such a compensation, he is in duty bound to serve for that day, but not otherwise. The condition of contract of hire requires that the return of profit be equal to the price of hire, and this cannot be ascertained but by degrees, and in course of time. The contract of hire, therefore, becomes complete, or fulfilled according to the services or benefit actually rendered in return for the price of hire received, and the person hired has consequently the option of dissolving the contract at any moment of the period originally agreed for.

"It is unavoidable and necessary in contracts of a different nature, such as in rent of land, &c., that the lessee should not have this power; but reverting to contracts of hire for service for a long period, the nefarious practices of subjecting free men to a state of bondage, under this pretence, it appears expedient to provide against such abuses; and with this view to restrict the period for service in all contracts of hired freemen to a month, or year, or the utmost to three years, as in cases of Ijanawugh, a form of endowment. It is customary also among the Zanane Towaf, to purchase female free children from their parents, or by engagements directly with the children themselves; exclusively of the illegality of such purchases, there is a further evil resulting from this practice, which is, the children are taught dancing and singing for others, and are also made prostitutes, which are extremely improper, and expressly forbidden by the law."

Remarks by this excellent judge.—"From the reply it is evident that, by the Mussulman law, no man can have the right of property over another human being except a Mussulman, and even he can acquire that right over an infidel only, inhabiting a country not under the power and control of the faithful; and that this right, which Mussulmans have over infidels fighting against the faith, is acquirable by Isteela, which means the entire subjugation of any subject of property by force of arms; the right of property, therefore, which one man may possess over another, is to be acquired, in the first instance, by Isteela. It follows that all persons in a state of bondage, over whom the right of property has not been obtained by Isteela, or the offspring of parents over whom the above right was not acquired, are, by the Mussulman law, free; and that it is the duty of the Hakim, respecting persons claiming their freedom, over whom the right of property derived from Isteela cannot be legally established or traced, to declare such persons of either sex free by a legal recorded decision, which shall secure to them the future enjoyment of that freedom.

"Slaves sold or given away by the Imaum, or the ghazee (victorious troops) who shared at the distribution, or if afterwards they become the property of another by inheritance, continue slaves under the different rights of purchase, donation, and heirship. It appears by the Mussulman law that the offspring of a female slave, whether by a freeman or a slave of any description, except by her master, such offsprings are slaves, and are called *khanazad* (born in the family). If, however, the offspring shall be acknowledged by the master, they shall be free, and the mother also, at the death of her owner, becomes free; *and this also emancipates their descendants to the latest posterity.* It may be inferred from the provision here noticed, &c., that, *to entitle the child to freedom, and the mother to emancipation, on the death of her lord, his acknowledgment, and that he is the father, the offspring of the slave is necessary to give the law force.* Here the principles pursued by European legislation are reversed, and there are many obvious motives that may induce the owner to deny his being the father of the child.

"It is declared by the Mussulman law, as here developed, that a *free man cannot sell his own person.* The law officer here states his unacquaintance with the circumstances which led to the prevalence of the custom in most Mussulman countries, of purchasing and selling the inhabitants of *Zanguibar*, *Ethiopia*, *Nubia*, and other *Negros:* they are evidently not legally slaves by the Mussulman law.

"Here is stated a custom existing amongst the Zanane Towaf, of purchasing female free born children from their parents or others, or making engagements with the children themselves, to be taught the practice of dancing and singing for others, and also for the purpose of being made prostitutes, which are allowed to be extremely improper and expressly forbidden by the law. *The extent of the above evil would be best ascertained by a few appropriate queries put to the several magistrates, but more especially to those of the large cities; the result would at once open the eyes of government to an evil which loudly calls for the interference of the Legislature, on every principle of humanity, morals, and policy.*"

Second Ques. "*What legal powers are the owners of slaves allowed to exercise upon the persons of their slaves, and particularly of their female slaves?*"

Ans. "The rightful proprietor of male and female slaves has a claim to the services of such slaves to the extent of their ability. He may employ them in baking, cooking, in making, dyeing, and washing clothes; as agents in mercantile transactions; in attending cattle, in tillage, or cultivation; as carpenters, ironmongers, and goldsmiths; in transcribing; as weavers, and in manufacturing woollen cloths; as shoemakers, boatmen, twisters of silk, water drawers; in shaving; in performing surgical operations, such as cupping, &c.; as farriers, bricklayers, and the like. He may hire them out on service in any of the above capacities; he may employ them himself, or for the use of his family in other duties of a domestic nature, such as in fetching water for washing on *evazoo* (religious purification), or anointing his body with oil, rubbing his feet, or attending his person while dressing, and in guarding the door of his house, &c. He may also have connexion with his legal female slave, provided she is arrived at the years of maturity, and the master or proprietor has not previously given her in marriage to another!"

" There is nothing objectionable in the duties here stated to be lawfully demanded from slaves of both sexes. The obvious immorality, and the great impolicy and inhumanity of the licentious authority stated in this answer, requires no comment. The law officer, although he has stated in part the truth, has not embraced the whole truth: the Islamite has the power, by the Mussulman law, of exercising with his female slaves, licentious intercourse, at the mention of which modesty recedes with blushes, and humanity shrinks with horror!"

Third Ques. "*What offences upon the persons of slaves, and particularly of female slaves, committed by their owners or by others, are legally punishable, and in what manner?*"

Ans. "If a master oppress his slave by employing him on any duty beyond his ability, as insisting upon his carrying a load which he is incapable of bearing, or climbing a tree which he cannot, the Hakim or ruling power may chastise him. It is also improper for a master to order his slave to do that which is forbidden by the law, such as putting an innocent person to death, setting fire to a house, tearing the clothes off another, or prostituting himself by adultery and fornication; to steal or drink spirits, or to slander and abuse the chaste and virtuous; and, if a master be guilty of such like oppressions, the Hakim may inflict exemplary punishment by *Fazir* and *Ucqubut Shukool Allah* (literally, the right of God), and meaning on principles of public justice.

"It is further unlawful for a master to punish his male or female slave for disrespectful conduct, and such like offences, further than by *sadeeb* (slight correction), as the power of passing sentence of *tazeer* and *gizes* is solely vested in the Hakim. If, therefore, the master should exceed the limits of his power of chastisement, above stated, he is liable to *tazeer*. If a master should have connexion with his female slave, before she has arrived at the years of maturity, and, if the female slave should in consequence be seriously injured, or should die, the ruling power may punish him by *tazeer* and *Ucqubut Hagool Jillah*, as before defined."

" It will be allowed, that the spirit which enumerates and limits the employments which a master is hereby forbidden to extort from his slaves, under the penalty of being liable to exemplary punishment by the Hakim, on principles of public justice, is humane, and might be sufficient for the purpose of good government, were it possible that the spirit of the law could be carried into effect. To any man acquainted with the manners and customs of the natives, no argument is necessary to prove that the reverse is the case. It is hardly necessary to remark on the degree of suffering that an illiterate, wretched, and desponding slave will submit to from his lord, whom, from infancy perhaps, he has been accustomed to look upon, with trembling anxiety, as the sole arbiter of his fate, upon whose pleasure all the little happiness, or rather the absence of misery, which he hopes to experience, entirely depends. Is it likely that a slave under such circumstances should dare to apply to the ruling power for redress?

"If a master, excited by lust, unrestrained by shame, or by habit, shall have connexion with a female slave before she has arrived at the years of maturity, if the female slave should in consequence be severely injured or die, what is the consequence? The ruling power may punish him as before defined. Shall a British government sanction so horrid a law?"

Fourth Ques. "*Are slaves entitled to emancipation upon any and what maltreatment, and may the courts of justice adjudge their emancipation upon the proof of such maltreatment? May such judgment be passed upon proof that a female slave has, during her minority, been prostituted by her master or mistress, or that any attempt of violence has been made by her owner?*"

Ans. "If the master of male or female slaves should tyrannize over them by treating them unjustly, stinting them in food, or imposing upon them duties of an oppressive nature; or if a master should have connexion with his slave girl before she has arrived at the years of maturity, or should give her in marriage to another, with permission to cohabit with her in this state, such master sins against the divine laws, and the ruling power may punish him; but the *commission of such crimes by the master does not authorize the manumission of the slave, nor has the Hakim any right or authority to grant emancipation.* Adverting to the principle upon which the legality of slavery is originally established, viz., *that the subject of property must be an infidel, and taken in the act of hostilities against the faith; and also to the several branches of legal slavery arising from this principle, as by purchase, donation, inheritance, and khanazadee;* whenever a case of possession of an unlawful male or female slave should be referred to the Hakim for investigation, it is his duty to pass an order, according to the original right of freedom of such individual, to deprive the unjust proprietor of possession, and to grant immediate emancipation to the slave.

(Signed and sealed)

Soorajoddeen Ullee,
Mahomed Rashed."

"The purport of this question is, whether on any or what maltreatment a slave is entitled to emancipation on proof, and whether the courts of justice are entitled to pass such judgment, particularly on females prostituted by their master or mistress during their minority, or on any attempt of violence being made. From the reply to this question, it appears that acts of oppression, and even violation of the person of a female slave, before she is at the years of maturity, by the master, or the crime of giving her at that age in marriage, are declared, as they truly are, crimes against the divine laws, and the ruling power may punish by stripes; but it is to be observed that, by the Mussulman law, the commission of these crimes by the owner does not entitle the wretched slave to manumission, nor has the ruling power a right to grant her emancipation ! !

"Humanity, which is shocked at the idea of its being a question whether or not British legislation shall sanction so diabolic a law, under the impressions of horror which every humane mind must feel at the depravity of such inhuman laws, is relieved by the perusal of the next sentence. Adverting to the principle upon which the legality of slavery is originally established, viz., *the subject of property must be an infidel taken in the act of hostilities against the faith*; and also to the several branches of legal slavery which shoot from this root or principle, —purchase, donation, inheritance, and khanazeed; whenever a case of possession of an unlawful male or female slave, that is to say, who is not himself or herself under the original description of an infidel taken in the act of hostilities against the faithful under an Imaum, or descended from a person of the above description, over whom the right of property has not been obtained by one of the modes described, shall come before the ruling power, to pass an order according to the original right of freedom of such individual, and to deprive the unjust proprietor of possession, and to grant an immediate emancipation."

Similar questions were put to the Hindoo Pundit by the Nizamut Adawlut.

First Ques. Ans. "There are *fifteen* different sorts of male and female slaves." See p. 11.

Remarks.—"Of the injustice and unreasonableness of the whole of the description of slaves sanctioned by the Hindoo law on the acknowledged principles of natural freedom, or on principles of expediency and humanity, few I conceive will doubt; and to enter into argument to prove this self-evident perversion of the laws of nature and of God, written in the hearts of all enlightened men, would be a waste of intellect. I am confident such wide-spread degradation of the human race can never be authorized by an enlightened British Government."

Second Ques. Ans. "The owner of a male or female slave may require of such slave the performance of impure work, such as plastering and sweeping the house, cleaning the door, gateway, and necessary; rubbing his master's naked body, *bunudome nehanu*, with oil, and clothing him; removing fragments of victuals left at his master's table, and eating them; removing urine and human ordure; rubbing his master's feet and other limbs, &c. In cases of disobedience or fault committed by the slave, the master has power to beat his slave with a thin stick, or to bind him with a rope: and, if he should consider the slave deserving of severe punishment, he may *pull his hair or expose him upon an ass;* but, if the master should exceed this extent of his authority, and inflict punishment upon his slave of a severer nature than above stated, he is liable to pay a fine to the Hakim or ruling power, of a thousand puns of *khar mahozrens,* eight thousand cowries.

This is declared by Menu, according to Patnakar Behbab, Chinta, Munnie, and other authorities."

"The facility and impunity with which power can tyrannize over a wretch in a state of bondage and absolute dependence is evident; and what is the punishment if, against all chance of hope, the tyrant is brought to trial, and even to conviction? A pecuniary fine!"

Third Ques. Ans. "A master has no right to command his male or female slave to perform any other duties besides those specified in the answer to the second question, or authority to punish his slave further than in the manner before stated; and if he should exceed this discretionary power, in either case, he is liable to the same penalty, viz. one thousand puns of cowries. This is declared by Menu and Beshie."

Fourth Ques. Ans. "The commission of offences, of the above nature by the master, does not affect the state of the slave; and the ruling power has not the right of granting his manumission. But if it should be established in evidence, before the Hakim, that any person having stolen or inveigled away, a child or slave, had afterwards sold him to another, or that any person had compelled another into a state of slavery by violence, the ruling power may then order the emancipation of such child or slave; and if a master, or any other person by permission of the master, should cohabit with a slave girl before she has arrived at the years of maturity, and this fact be proved, the ruling power may sentence such offender to pay a fine of *fifty puns* of cowries, but cannot emancipate the slave girl!

"Whenever a slave girl has borne a child by her master, *such slave, together with the child, becomes free, and the ruling power should sanction their emancipation.*

"This is the law declared by Jak Bulk Mannoo and Kutoobun, according to Mittuchora and other authorities.

(Signed) *Chattoor Bhooj Necarutun,*
Chiterput Oapadhea."

"It does not appear that the commission of any, or all of the offences supposed in the fourth question, affect the state of bondage in the sufferings of the wretched slave, nor by the Hindoo law has the ruling power the authority of emancipating the injured bondsman, even under all the above maltreatment; but a treacherous inveigling away of a child and selling it as a slave, or subjecting to slavery by violence, are declared illegal, and the ruling power may emancipate such child or slave. Should, however, a master, or any other by permission of the owner, cohabit with a slave girl before she has arrived at the years of maturity, and the fact be proved, the ruling power may sentence the offender to *fifty puns of cowries!* Here a crime, most monstrous, by which the laws of nature are outraged, is punishable by a pecuniary fine! I suppose for the benefit of the ruling power."

"The foregoing being the Mussulman law, as expounded by the law officers, and that law being it by which we govern in cases of life and limb, surely it ought to be extended to personal freedom; for from it alone can life or limb, the first gifts of nature, acquire their due value. The foregoing, I think, will be admitted, and investigation will render it evident, that *at the present moment, of the many thousands male and female slaves held in bondage in the Company's dominions, and subject to the grossest usage, prostitution, and every other depravity, under the pretence of slavery being sanctioned by the Mussulman law, not a single man or woman exists, to whom the right of property, on the principle laid down by that law, can possibly be established!* The mode, therefore, of remedying the gross evils that exist, is as easy as it is obvious. Enforce the spirit and letter of the Mussulman law as it applies to slaves, and as far as that portion of the inhabitants of our Indian possessions are concerned, you remedy the evil, and give the blessing of liberty to thousands, without infringing a particle of the Mahomedan religion; on the contrary, so far as this regulation is connected with it, you only check a licentious deviation from the principles of law and religion on the point in question."*

The practice of kidnapping children, for the purpose of selling them as slaves, appears to have been very prevalent in various parts of India. Respecting a case of this kind at *Midnapore*, on the borders of Orissa, in 1794, the Magistrate, R. Bathurst, Esq., thus expressed his indignation of the crime.—"To that part of the futwa which respects Shazaddee, equity and humanity alike prompt me to object in the strongest terms. Her crime is *of a nature, to break asunder the tenderest ties, and to consign its innocent victims, either rudely torn or cruelly seduced from their parents' home, to hopeless slavery; to experience in the course of it, too probably, no wages but stripes, no relief but death.* Such is the complexion of her guilt. What says the futwa, which, regulated by Mussulman justice, weighs, it would seem, in the same scale of moral turpitude, the stealing of a cur dog and the kidnapping of a child? Thirty-five strokes with a rattan and four months' confinement, which if changed to hard labour and imprisonment for life, although still disproportioned to the extent of her offence, might, perhaps, operate to deter others from the practice of similar enormities."†

* Par. Papers on Slavery in India, 1828, pp. 309—317.

† Par. Papers, p. 52. See also pp. 242, 243.

The nature of slavery in *Canara*, under the Madras Presidency, is thus described by J. G. Ravenshaw, Esq., Collector, in 1801.

"There are three distinctions of the daerds or slaves,—*the moondaul, mogare*, or magor, *and mavey;* the two former differ from the latter in the way of food;—neither of them will eat the flesh of a cow or bullock; or go near the place where one has died or been killed, till the carcase has been removed; the mavey daerd, though he will not kill the animal, will eat its flesh after it is dead. If one dies at the house of a moondaul or magor, a mavey is sent for to remove the carcase. In the moondaul and mayer sects, property descends from uncle to nephew; *a father gives up his children to their uncle.* In the mogare sects, property descends from father to son. A mogare and a moondaul will eat together, though it is not common; if, however, they do, the form of taking away the dishes or pans they eat out of, washing and returning them clean to the party who gives the repast, is invariably observed. They never intermarry by consent; but if a moondaul runs away with a mogare, the latter sect assemble, call on the moondaul, and, after reprimanding him for the crime he has committed, make him pay a fine for the offence, and give a repast to the whole party; when they have eaten, the mogare is considered as having relinquished her cast, and being made over to the moondaul. Neither of these sects associate with the mavey daerd.

"If a *moondaul* goes to a landlord, or other person, and says he wants to marry through his interests; if the person consents, he gives him from three to four pagodas to pay the expense of the ceremony; the daerd, as soon as married, brings his wife to his landlord's house, and both are bound to serve him and his heirs as long as the husband lives. The landlord is considered as bound to give the man, per annum, two cloths, each five cubits in length; and the woman two, each of eight cubits length, one to cover the lower and one the upper part of their frame, the estimated expense of which is one and a half rupees; the man is to receive one and a half, and the woman one hami of rice per diem, besides one mora of rice per annum between them; this allowance is called '*mogu*.' This couple have *no claim over any children they may have born: they are the exclusive property of their uncle.* If he agree to their remaining with their father till they are grown up, and their father consents to keep them, this may be done; and if, when grown up, their father's owner gives the males money to marry, they are bound to serve him and his heirs as long as they live. If, however, their uncle does not agree to their remaining with their father when young, he takes them, and his master pays them according to the work they do. As to the daughters, if their uncle agree, they may remain with their father, till some person comes with their uncle's consent to ask them in marriage; they are then given up and bound to serve their husband's owner. In the event of the husband's death, his master has no right whatever over the mother and children, who become the property of, or for whom the children's uncle is bound to provide, and they are bound to serve his master if he has work for them. If a man wants to marry a second time, his master supplies him with money; in consideration of this extra expense, he stops the '*mogu*,' or allowance of one mora of rice per annum. A man receives no daily allowance for himself and family during his master's harvest, but, in lieu thereof, he gets an *eleventh part of as much grain as is cut, thrashed, and stacked by the whole of them;* when this work is done, they receive their daily subsistence as usual. The sect may be called *a life property on the male side*; they are never sold, though they sometimes mortgage themselves, and their owners may also mortgage them.

"The *mogare* are bought and sold, and hence *they and their male heirs are bound to serve their master and his heirs for ever.* Females remain with their fathers till married, after which their owners have no claim on them; they become the property of their husband's master. The average price of a man and his wife, if purchased together, is *from four to five pagodas.* These mogairs receive the same daily allowance of rice and cloth as the moondauls, but they get no annual allowance, the piece of land and the two trees they get are supposed more than to equal this; and in addition to it, if their master can afford it, he frequently gives them a bullock. The owner pays only as many of the family as work for him. This sect are sometimes mortgaged, as well as sold.

"If a person purchases a man and woman of the *mauray sect*, and marries them, they and their male heirs are bound to serve him and his heirs for ever; the purchaser pays the expense of the marriage. If the man dies, and the woman marries again, *the children she may have by her new husband are all the property of her owner*, by reason of his having purchased the woman; but he has no claim whatever on the new husband. When these people are not purchased, but merely bind themselves to the service, on account of some person having paid the expense of their marriages, as the moondauls do, the same rules are observed as with them; but there are many of these sects, who belonging, or being, as it were, an appurtenant to an estate, are bought and sold therewith; they enjoy the same privileges and allowances as those of the same sect who are purchased without an estate. The landlord can neither sell nor mortgage them, nor can they, without the landlord's consent, mortgage themselves or children. In many of the foregoing cases, an owner is bound to give daily subsistence to as many only of the family of his slaves as he employs; if he has more than he requires, he may lend them out to other people, who pay him the mogu, or annual allowance of one mora of rice, as a sort of acknowledgment that the daerd he employs belongs to him. Daerds cannot go to work for another person without their owners' consent, and they are bound to return whenever he may have work for them."*

"The utmost to which the sale of slaves is tolerated in *Malabar*," says J. H. Baber, Esq., Judge and Magistrate in the North Zilla in 1812, "is domestic slavery, and this is exclusively confined to those born in a state of bondage. Formerly this degraded race of men were the exclusive property of the Hindoos of Malabar, but in course of time, from necessity and other causes, they were transferred and sold to the Mopillas, but it was never bargained that they were to be made proselytes. A Pooliar sold or transferred could not be removed out of the district, his place of nativity; in consequence of the social tie amongst them was still preserved; even the women, though sold, are never separated from their husbands, whom they still follow, however often they may change their masters; the owner of the female, however, *still maintaining his claim to her and to her offspring, whose right is thus perpetuated from generation to generation.* In some districts, *the offspring are* DIVIDED *between the owners of the father and the mother, but they are never separated from their parents until adults.*"†

The evils of slavery are innumerable. "To remedy the evil," says one of the Judges in India, "it appeared to me highly necessary that it should be ascertained and acknowledged, and its extent fully understood."‡ The propriety of

* Par. Papers on Slavery in India, pp. 548—550.

† p. 567. See p. 897. This state of society is prevalent in the Indian Archipelago. See a description of Malay Slavery by the Acting President of *Fort Marlborough* in 1813. Par. Papers, pp. 203—205.

‡ Par. Papers, p. 308.

this appears from the want of information respecting slavery in India. The following extracts from the valuable Papers on this subject, it is hoped will rouse the attention of Britain, to the state of slavery in her eastern dominions.

"No progress in arts or science can be expected," says the worthy Judge of *Bundlecund*, "from unhappy beings whose daily reflections press their forlorn condition upon their thoughts. The rudest cultivation of the earth is performed with reluctance, by wretches whose miseries know no end, but in the moments of repose. Perhaps exposed to the burning heat of a vertical sun, immerged to the knees in water, stagnate and unwholesome, respiring a vapour inimical to existence; perhaps buried alive in mines replete with noxious minerals and baneful air, which slowly consumes the human frame. Or if (which is the summit of a slave's good fortune) they meet with a more lenient lord, still their comforts are embittered by the dread of a change. The stroke of death, or the pressure of misfortune, may transfer them with their former master's cattle or his lands, to a less tender lord; devoid of any established mode of providing for, or bringing up a family, and fearful of entering into the marriage state, having no protection or security that their dearest and most tender connexions will not be set at nought by the capricious lust of pampered power, population suffers.

"In Hindostan slaves are kept for show, or employed in the meanest and most laborious offices of servitude. In ancient times slaves were bred to trades; to cultivate the sciences and other philosophic studies, and some of this class distinguished themselves by their abilities, and contributed to enlighten mankind. But how much more speedily has general improvement increased, since the establishment of freedom through the principal parts of Europe. The freest nations have ever been the first to dispel the clouds of error, and brighten the dawnings of knowledge into the meridian splendour of truth. If any thing can add to the horror which the idea of slavery raises in every human breast, it is the reflection that, by the Mussulman law respecting female slaves, the master is not only legal lord of their persons for purposes of laborious services, but for sensual gratification; even such as his unnatural passions may impel his brutality to indulge. It is not less shocking to reflect that women, who have spent their youth and worn out their persons in the grossest debauchery, when their faded beauty no longer produces their wonted luxuries, and even their former paramours in guilt turn from them with disgust, purchase female children for the avowed purpose of the most licentious life. These females, were such injurious practices prevented by *the abolition of all slavery*, would become useful members of the community, and add to the prosperity of the state. Under systematic slavery the minds of mankind are inevitably debased. Children being educated amongst these wretches, imbibe their dispositions, and, having the examples of their parents always before their eyes, learn to consider those under them as a distinct race, unworthy of the rights of humanity. The first efforts of imitative cruelty are viewed by the parents without reprehension, their own minds having undergone the same perversion by the same tuition, and the practice of maturity having deadened their feelings; so that I fear, not unfrequently, this early discovery of vicious inclination is considered by the fond, but mistaken parent, as a sure presage of spirit and future greatness. View the manners of those nations who tolerate slavery, and say whether this reasoning is not warranted by reality."*

F. Lascelles, third Judge in *Tinnevelly* in 1832, describing the four kinds of slaves, very feelingly observes :—"The third class, dancing girls, is by far the most objectionable, combining as it does, every attendant on the very worst description of slavery. Initiated in early youth into the mysteries of their profession, and immured within the walls of the pagoda, they are taught as their first and chief lesson, to consider an implicit obedience to the will of the Brahmin as their highest duty. Their servile compliance with the disgusting desires of their superiors rob them of all self-respect. The aged are seldom found among this wretched class, nor is it possible in many cases to trace their steps! I believe it to be a well known fact, that there is a large class of men who obtain a livelihood by traffic in female children, *for the use of the pagodas;* and although it does not appear that any violence is used in carrying on this nefarious practice, yet perhaps there never existed any system more truly injurious to the morals of the people, or one which so loudly calls for correction."† What a description is this of the Hindoo temples, but how fully in accordance with the character of those of antiquity—"*Nam quo non prostrat fœmina templo.*"—*Juv.*

Sir William Jones, in a charge to the grand jury at *Calcutta*, in 1785, described the miseries of slavery existing at

* Par. Papers on Slavery in India, 1828, pp. 298—300.

† Par. Papers, 1838, p. 392.

that period, even in the metropolis of British India. "I am assured, from evidence which, though not all judicially taken, has the strongest hold on my belief, that the condition of slaves within our jurisdiction is, beyond imagination, deplorable; and that cruelties are daily practised on them, chiefly on those of the tenderest age and the weaker sex, which, if it would not give me pain to repeat, and you to hear, yet, for the honour of human nature, I should forbear to particularize. If I except the English from this censure, it is not through partial affection to my own countrymen, but because my information relates chiefly to people of other nations, who likewise call themselves Christians. Hardly a man or a woman exists in a corner of this populous town, who hath not at least one slave child, either purchased at a trifling price, or saved, perhaps, from a death that might have been fortunate, for a life that seldom fails of being miserable. Many of you, I presume, have seen *large boats filled with such children, coming down the river for open sale at Calcutta*; nor can you be ignorant that most of them were stolen from their parents, or bought, perhaps, for a measure of rice in a time of scarcity; and that the sale itself is a defiance of this government, by violating one of its positive orders, which was made some years ago, after a consultation of the most reputable Hindoos in Calcutta, who condemned such a traffic as repugnant to their shastra. The number of small houses, in which these victims are pent, makes it indeed very difficult for the settlement at large to be apprized of their condition; and, if the sufferers knew where or how to complain, their very complaints may expose them to still harsher treatment—*to be tortured, if remanded, or if set at liberty, to starve.* Be not discouraged by the difficulty of your inquiries; your vigilance cannot but surmount it; and one great example of a just punishment, not capital, will conduce more to the prevention of similar cruelties, than the strongest admonition or the severest verbal reproof. Should the slave-holders, through hardness of heart, or confidence in their places of concealment, persist in their crimes, you will convince them, that their punishment will certainly follow their offence, and the most hardened of them will, no doubt, discontinue the contest."

In 1810, a claim was preferred before the court of Sudder Dewanny Adawlut, for the restoration of some slaves who had escaped from *Nepaul*, and sought an asylum in the British territory. Nine slaves were stated to have been purchased for 226 rupees. This sum was given by the British Government, and the slaves liberated. The depositions of two or three of them show *the nature of slavery in Nepaul.*

"Jeewee acknowledged that he was a slave, but alleged that, being employed in cultivating, and receiving nothing from the prosecutor, he had run away. He represented that, *if he should now return to the hills, the prosecutor would cut off his ears as a punishment for his offence!*

"Dhunsree acknowledged that she was the slave of the prosecutor, saying, that she *having killed her own child, was brought by the prosecutor* before Meer Singh Tuppa, who gave her to him *to keep as his slave,* that *this was the usual punishment for murder in the hilly country:* she added, that, having received nothing from the prosecutor to eat, she had run off.

"Joonhee and Lamee also acknowledged that they were slaves, and alleged the same reason for having run away from the prosecutor.

"Oodhree, witness, deposed that Meer Singh Tuppa had given Nathee and Dhunsree to the prosecutor's son as payment of his monthly allowance; that Nathee had formerly been the slave of Shoobur Suen, and that Dhrunsee *having killed her own child,* had been given by Meer Singh Tuppa to the prosecutor, whose slave she had now been for three years. With respect to the other four persons, the prosecutor not having given them any present, they had therefore run off. He further stated, that, *it was the custom of the hill country, that if any woman put to death her new-born infant, she was reduced to slavery by the ruler; but, if she be able to give her value to her master, he may free her; and, in case of a dispute regarding the amount of the purchase money, it is to be settled on the oath of the master.*" It is added, "that if the slaves were delivered to the prosecutor, *he would certainly put them to death, on getting them to their own country.*"*

The misery of arbitrary servitude is depicted in a very affecting manner, relative to thirty-five natives of Bengal, who, in 1813, were found in the service of Mr. W. Browne, at *Sydney, New South Wales;* they were discharged by the colonial magistrates, and restored to their native country, at the expense of the British Government.† Three of their depositions before the magistrate are given.

"Chotee Lutchman, servant of Mr. Browne—I complain of want of food; I sometimes got rice, sometimes ottar and wheat, and dhal and corn, the same as the rest; I have been ill-treated while I was employed in the store. Mr. O'Brien *tied a rope to me to awake me in case of alarm:* I did not like it, and objected to it; Mr. O'Brien persisted in it, and then he gave me a rope's-ending. I used to do all sorts of work for him; I got a thrashing for throwing some straw out, which offended Mr. O'Brien, in consequence of which I went up to the farm; Mr. Browne ordered me back to Sydney, but as it rained he allowed me to remain till next day. I got drunk, for which Mr. Browne put me for three days on short allowance. I ran away in the bush; I was not flogged for it. I have worked on Sundays for myself; if the others go home, I want to go also, but if they stop I will not. I had two bottles of rum charged to me; it was watered. I have lost my caste for eating victuals of Europeans, because I could get nothing else.

"The memorial of Chamine Dongrine, and of Charon Munny, respectfully showeth:—

* Par. Papers on Slavery in India, pp. 119, 120. See pp. 243, 244.
† See pp. 267—296.

"That both memorialists engaged with Mrs. Browne, of Calcutta, to serve her in New South Wales, and have both been employed on her farm; but, by reason of cruelty and ill-usage on their mistress's part, they pray humbly, but earnestly, to be released from such agreement. The former memorialist has to complain, that she was employed at field labour, such as commonly is done by men in this colony; and, having been put to bed of a male infant, she was ordered to return to work by Mrs. Browne, *on the fifth day after the child was born!* Upon remonstrating that she was not sufficiently strong, Mrs. Browne withheld her victuals; thereby compelling her to go reaping wheat, the infant lying on the ground of the storeroom locked up, *which occasioned its death at twenty-one days old, for want of milk!*

"Your memorialist, Charon Munny, has to represent, amongst a continual length of ill-treatment, that, having been forced to carry a large brazen vessel of great weight, she then being heavy with child, miscarried; *the next day*, Mrs. Browne ordered her to work, such as carrying large logs, and other loads. Relying fully on the justice and humanity which distinguish every court under British administration, your petitioners submit their hardships to your consideration, should the same appear to require such redress as they ask."*

Of the state of slavery in *Malwa*, in 1821, Sir John Malcolm observes,—"Male slaves are few in Malwa, and are generally treated more like adopted children than menials. The case is very different with females, who in almost every instance are sold to prostitution; some, it is true, rise to be favourite mistresses of their master, while others are raised by the success in life of their sons; but these are exceptions. The dancing women, who are all slaves, are condemned to a life of toil and vice, for the profit of others, and some of the first Rajpoot chiefs and zemindars in Malwa, have from 50 to 200 female slaves in their family. After employing them in the menial labours of their house during the day, they send them at night to their own dwellings, where they are at liberty to form such connexions as they please; but a large share of the profits of that promiscuous intercourse, into which they fall, is annually exacted by their masters, who add any children they have to their list of slaves. The female slaves in this condition, as well as those of the dancing sets, are not permitted to marry, and are often very harshly treated; so that the latter, from this cause, and the connexions they form, are constantly in the habit of running away. If discovered, they are always given up, provided the deed of purchase can be produced; which with them, above all others, must be registered at the cutwall's chabootre, at the period the slave is bought. It is not the habit of the native governments of Malwa, to take any cognizance of the punishment which masters inflict upon slaves, except such extend to their life, when they are responsible; they are in some cases cruelly treated, but this is not general; it is indeed against the inter-

* Par. Papers on Slavery, pp. 274—276, 281.

est of the master to do so, when there are so many opportunities of escaping from his authority. The state of Malwa for the last thirty years has been favorable to the species of slavery described, and that province is filled with the mixed progeny of these unfortunate women. This traffic must however now decrease, as the Gwarriahs and others who carried it on, can no longer steal or conceal children with that confidence of impunity which they had long done. A few years ago, no man dare leave his own district to inquire after his wife and daughter; the whole country can now be traversed in safety. From this cause, and the discoveries of guilt which have recently been made, the stealers of women and children have taken alarm; while the restitution to their relatives of slaves, bought by them at high prices, must deter future purchasers."*

Slavery in *Malacca,* in 1829, is thus characterized;—"That the subscribers to the slave petition should speak of the 'comforts' which the slaves forfeit by seeking their liberty, and should declare that these people have been treated more as children than slaves, is not surprising—they speak of themselves! Before I can subscribe to such an opinion, I must cast from my mind the remembrance of the cries which I have heard, and the mental degradation, the rags, the wretchedness, the bruises, the contused eyes, and burns which I have witnessed. I must blot adultery from the calendar of vices; I must disbelieve the numerous proofs which I have had of obstacles opposed to regular marriages, and the general humiliation of the females. I must put away every idea of the modes of punishment of which eye-witnesses have given me account, and the short jacket must no longer be deemed a peculiar badge of slavery."†

The evils of slavery in the Island of *Nias,* near *Sumatra,* are forcibly depicted in an article from the *Singapore Chronicle;*—

"The circumstances that attend the traffic of slaves are no less revolting to humanity, than those which marked it on the coast of Africa. The unhappy victims, torn by violence from their friends and country, are delivered, pinioned hand and foot, to the dealers in human flesh, are kept bound during the whole course of the voyage—a precaution which is found necessay to the safety of the crew. Instances have occurred, where the captives have seized a moment of liberty, to snatch up the first weapon within their reach, stab all whom they encountered, and complete the scene by leaping overboard, and voluntarily seeking a watery death! The sudden change of diet to which they are subjected on board a ship, added *to the confinement and dejection of mind, prove fatal to many!*

* Par. Papers, pp. 415, 416.

† Par. Papers, 1838, p, 270.

Of a cargo of *thirty* slaves, *twenty* have been known to perish before the conclusion of the voyage; and on a moderate calculation it may be estimated, that, of the total number purchased, *one-fourth* never reach their destination.

"On the scenes of violence that take place in the country itself, in the search of victims, it is needless to dwell; they can be better imagined than described. We shall relate one well authenticated instance, given by an eye-witness. A plan had been laid to attack a single insulated house, inhabited by a man, his wife, and children, and to seize the whole family. At the appointed hour the house was surrounded; the man no sooner discovered his situation, and saw that there was no escape, than he locked himself in the inner apartment, drew his *kris*, killed first his wife and children, and then plunged it into his own breast, preferring death to a life of slavery!!

"Independently of the habits of cruelty and rapine, which the slave-trade tends to infuse, the exorbitant profits it holds out, create an aversion to the slower advantages of legitimate commerce and agricultural labour. In order to convey their produce to the sea-ports, the inhabitants of the interior are obliged to unite in parties of several hundreds, all completely armed, and, with their loads of rice upon their backs, descend in order of battle to the shores to dispose of it; such is the general insecurity and distrust, that the husbandman goes armed to his labour in the fields, they select the most difficult situations for their villages, and construct their houses with every precaution against surprises."*

"Nothing can be more abject and wretched (says T. H. Baber, Esq., Magistrate of *Malabar*, in 1813,) than the condition of that degraded race of mortals, the slaves of Malabar, '*whose huts* (to use the words of Mr. Francis Buchanan, in his tour through Malabar), *are little better than mere baskets, and whose diminutive stature, and squalid appearance, evidently show a want of adequate nourishment*."† This gentleman, in 1832, was led to make very similar remarks. "Since that time (1812), I have confined myself to occasional notices of the condition of the Malabar slaves, as often as my public attention has been drawn to the subject, but with little or no benefit to the unfortunate slaves; who continue the same reprobated people as ever, as their half-famished persons, their sieves of huts, and the diminution of their numbers (while every other class of the people is increasing) abundantly testify."‡

"The slave alone (says Mr. Græme, in his Report of *Malabar*, 1822), has his *sieve of a hut* in the centre of the rice lands; but on the coast, at least, he is an industrious, and not an unintelligent being, in good condition, and nothing deficient in bodily frame. In the interior, *he is a wretched, half-starved, diminutive creature, stinted in his food, and exposed to the inclemencies of the weather; whose state demands*

* See Imp. Mag., Jan. 1830.—For an account of the misery of slavery in the *Isle of France*, see Memoir of Mrs. Judson, p. 81, respecting a Burmese female slave; see also p. 306.

† Par. Papers, pp. 760, 761.

‡ Par. Papers, 1832, p. 570. See also Par. Papers, 1830, p. 210.

that commiseration and melioration which may confidently be expected from the humanity of the British Government. Provided it can be shown, that a change for the better can be effected without hazarding an evil of any formidable magnitude; without incurring the risk of general discontent, or exciting a worse feeling towards the objects themselves, by an unsuccessful endeavour to mitigate their ill treatment. The slaves of Malabar, known generally by the name of *chermurs*, are *entirely prædial, or rustic*, being engaged only in the cultivation of rice lands and plantations. I except, of course, the Mussulmans, who may be domestic slaves, and live in the houses of their masters, and partake of all the privileges of their religion. This kind of slavery is a social fraternity, and is a step to the best comforts and the highest honours of life among Mussulmans. It is totally dissimilar, in every essential point, to the servitude of the chermur, which is the most prevalent designation of the slaves of Malabar."*

A. D. Campbell, Esq., in his reply to the questions on slavery by the Board of Control, in 1832, feelingly acknowledges, "The creatures in human form who constitute, to the number of 100,000, the agrestic slave population of Malabar, being distinguishable, like the savage tribes still to be found in some of the forests of Arabia, from the rest of the human race, *by their degraded, diminutive, squalid appearance, their dropsical, pot bellies*, contrasting horribly with their *skeleton arms and legs, half starved, hardly clothed, and in a condition scarcely superior to the cattle they follow at the plough!* I am by no means satisfied that due provision is made for the support of agrestic slaves in sickness or in old age. Their masters are bound to support them; but in the absence of any summary means to enforce the obligation, I fear the poor and infirm slave is often left to the doubtful remedy of a law suit against his master, or to the uncertain charity of his brethren stinted in their own means."†

"In the Calicut District, there is an anomaly in the general system among the Paliur, the Kulladee, and the Kunnakur, which are the only three casts of slaves residing there. There is a mixture of the two customs of *mukkatayum* and *murroo mukkatayum*, that is, the one or the other does not obtain separately in different families in the district, but in all the families throughout the district the inheritance partakes of the two modes; and *half the children are considered to go with the mother, and to belong to her proprietor, and half to be*

* Par. Papers, 1828, p. 914.

† Par. Papers, 1832, p. 574.

attached to the father, and to be the property of his master. Where the number may not admit of an equal division, the odd number is reckoned to be the mother's! The wife of a Palium, and of all the casts who observe the *murroo mukkatayum,* may be sold separately, and may therefore belong to a different master, from the master of her husband, but she cannot be separated from her husband; she must be allowed to remain with him; she is purchased separately in consideration of her future offspring, which, by the custom of *murroo mukkatayum, would become the property of her purchaser.* In the other casts, the females are not separately saleable, neither the wife nor her female children. The daughters become the temporary property of the masters of their husbands; but this right of property ceases upon the death of the husband, and the wife returns to the house of her father. The rules of Malabar prescribe that a slave of the cast of Poleyan, Waloovan, and Brayen, shall remain *seventy-two* paces from a Brahmin and from a Nair, and *forty-eight* from a Tean. A slave of the Kunakur cast, *sixty-four* paces from a Brahmin and Nair, and *forty* from a Tean; and the other casts generally *forty-eight* paces from a Brahmin and Nair, *twenty-four* from a Tean! In the northern division these rules are deviated from in practice, in favour of the slaves; whilst in the southern division, *they are thought to be exceeded in strictness.*"*

This absurd and cruel custom is thus described in the following account of a poor slave taking his child for medical advice: "He and his child went down by water, though it was with some difficulty that I got the boatmen, my own people, to admit them into my own boat. On returning from Tellicherry, they were obliged to come by land, and this poor pooliar and his infant have been one whole day in finding their way back, a distance of twelve miles, compelled, whenever they came in sight of a habitation, to fly from the public road, and make a long circuit to avoid the remotest approach. They were forced to utter a cry at almost every step they took, to give warning that a human being, and not a dog, was coming; and driven, whenever their cry was answered, to hide themselves in the jungle, until their superior, probably a fisherman, or saltmaker, had passed! Thus it is that the right of public way, which is freely conceded to every beast of the field, is denied to a whole class of human beings. This horrible tyranny is a remnant of that which the higher casts formerly exercised upon the lower; but as the British Government has

* Par. Papers, 1828, p. 920. See E. I. Mag., 1834, p. 244—252.

never tolerated it in the instance of the other casts, I most earnestly beg its authority may be rigorously interposed, *to withdraw the unhappy pooliar from a condition which ranks him beneath the lowest brute, and is, I believe, without a parallel in the annals of human abjectness and degradation*."*
—Aug., 1832.

One of the Malabar Magistrates, in 1823, suggested that, on account of "certain instances of cruelty practised on slaves by their masters, the forfeiture of the right of property over slaves should be made the penalty for ill usage."—Slaves appear occasionally to have their noses cut off by their cruel masters. "Adverting (says one of the Judges) to the facts elicited during the foregoing trial, *it will no longer be denied that cruelties are practised upon the slaves of Malabar;* and that our courts and cutcherries are no restraints upon their owners or employers. Whatever doubts may exist with regard to the exact period of the death of the Cherooman Koory Noryady, or to the immediate cause of his death, there can be none as to the fact, of *his nose having been amputated, as well as those of three other slaves belonging to the same owner;* and that, although the case had come before the Magistrate, no steps have been taken to bring the perpetrators of such horrid barbarities to justice. Upon the latter head it may be argued that the slaves themselves preferred no complaint: but, if it is to depend upon the slaves to seek for the protection of the laws, their situation must be hopeless indeed; for, having no means of subsistence, independent of their owners or employers, their repairing to and attending upon a public cutchery is impossible. Even though those provisions of the regulations, that require all complaints to be preferred in writing, were dispensed with in favour of slaves, and they were exempted from the payment of tolls at the numerous ferries they would have to pass, and though an allowance were made to them by government during their detention at the cutcherries and courts, unless *forfeiture of the right of property over slaves* was the penalty for ill usage, their situation would only become more intolerable than it was before they complained."†

"In *Malabar*, (says the Foujdaree Adawlut, of Madras, in 1829,) where the slave is often sold separately from the land, civilization is checked by the infraction of those feelings, the cultivation of which principally tends to raise human nature. *He is dragged from the field which he is accustomed to till, from all the connexions of blood and affection, and his*

* Par. Papers, 1838, pp. 413, 419, 420. † Par. Papers on Slavery, 1828, p. 928.

diminutive size, stinted growth, and squalid appearance, present the picture of the degrading being which he feels he is."*

The last page but one of the Par. Papers, 1828, contain the following remarks respecting the misery of slavery in British India. "The second Judge makes mention of two cases tried in Canara, wherein the accused were charged with causing the death of their slaves by severe chastisement, which, he states, induced him to make inquiry at *Mangalore*, regarding the prevailing custom in instances where the slave of one master marries the slave of another; and particularly whether their respective owners can prevent them from living together. The second Judge remarks that the frequent absence from his 'master's work, which occasioned the deeeased's chastisement in one of the above cases, was owing to visits to his wife, who resided at a distance on her master's estate, *who would not allow her to live with her husband.*' He was told that it is usual for the female slave to reside with her husband, and if his residence be at such a distance as to prevent her from coming to work daily at her master's house, the master of the husband must indemnify her owner by the payment, annually, of half a mora of rice; but, if the master should employ the female at his own house, he must employ also her husband, whose owner he must indemnify by the payment, annually, of one mora of rice. The Judge offers his opinion that the Magistrate should correctly inform himself on this point, and be required under the authority of Government, after due notice given, to enforce the obligation on the part of the owners, to allow their married slaves to live together. The court of Foujdaree Adawlut are of opinion, that the interference here proposed to be exercised by the Magistrate, could not be put in practice without the enactment of a Regulation for that purpose; and they are not prepared to suggest provisions with this view which would be free from objection; should, however, the Honorable the Governor in council deem it fit to give effect to the humane recommendation of the Judge, it may be in the power of the provincial court, in communication with the Magistrates in the provinces of *Malabar* and *Canara, to devise a mode to prevent the separation of married slaves, without any violation of rights, which the established usages in this respect confer.*"†

The degraded nature of their Idolatry is thus described by J. H. Baber, Esq :—

"Hindoo slaves, like their free countrymen, worship a variety of gods and god-

* Par. Papers, 1838, p. 404.

† Par. Papers on Slavery in India, 1828, pp. 935, 936.

desses, which are represented by rude *stones, logs of wood, or pottery.* They are placed on a pedestal or stool, on hearths or pavements, in the open air, or under cover, under the shade of the *alipoola*, or kamjera trees; some are inclosed within walls. In those of the higher casts, an image of granite stone is placed, upon which oil is poured; it is also decked with flowers. On many of these peetrims or altars, there is nothing but a *tre-shola*, trident of iron, or walla, a sword, and generally a curved one. Every mountain, hill, forest, field, river, &c., has its appropriate deity. Their officiating priests are persons of their own cast respectively. At particular ceremonies they have lights and beat drums, and sacrifice fowls, and make offerings of meal, meat, rice, nuts, honey, and spirituous liquors, to propitiate evil spirits, mediators, souls or spirits of departed relatives; also, to the protecting deities of their country. Their ideas of a future state of rewards and punishments is, that bad men become evil spirits, while good men continue to hover about their earthly dwellings. Some believe in transmigration: they have also some confused notions of a place of torment, called *naragum*, and of beatitude, called *sirargum*."*

This chapter may be closed, by contrasting "the effects of slavery with those of voluntary servitude, under a system of liberty," as described by the excellent Judge of Bundlecund.

SLAVERY.	VOLUNTARY SERVITUDE.
"1. It is the constant object of the master, to get the greatest quantity of labour at the cheapest rate; consequently he stints the slave in food and raiment. It may be urged, by clothing and feeding well, the slave would be strong, and better able to endure fatigue, but it is the constant practice of avarice, by short-sighted policy, to counteract its own wishes: a trifling immediate advantage being generally preferred to much more essential objects, if more remote.	1. The same object actuates the master here also, but the servant being free to stipulate, his interest counteracts that of the other, and the contest reduces and establishes the price of labour to its just rate; that is, it allows the servant to provide for himself and family, and leaves the master a competent profit.
2. It is the uniform endeavour of the slave to mitigate the hardship of his lot by evading toil, which brings him no advantage.	2. It is the general wish of servants to satisfy their masters, that they may not lose their employment; or, if their services are no longer requisite, to entitle them to a recommendation.
3. The slave, finding himself subject to capricious treatment and change of masters, will seldom add the cares of providing for a family of children to his other woes, and consequently avoids marriage.	3. The servant, knowing he can dispose of his earnings as he pleases, and being provided with a fund for the provision of a wife, &c., will marry; thus the state reaps benefit by the increase of population.
4. In their old age, it is the master's interest to get rid of the feeble, who eat, but cannot labour; consequently, the worn down slave is neglected, and perishes for want of care, having no family or children to ease the pains of sickness, or prop the weakness of decline, by the soothing attention of filial duty!	4. Under voluntary servitude, by the time old age approaches, many have saved a little from the rewards of their services, to assist in softening the hardships of sickness and debility, &c.; and almost all, having married and added to the general stock of industry and riches, have some children to soothe the evening of life. Though this may

* Par. Papers, 1832, p. 561.

have little weight in the scale of political reasoning, it ought to have some in that of humanity.

5. In times of scarcity and famine, the master must starve his slaves, send them to plunder, or emancipate them. The latter, his avarice will never permit.

5. In scarcity, a servant is not more difficult to subsist than a slave; he will not eat more, and, having his wages, he is better enabled to evade the effects of famine, by making timely provision for its approach.

6. When slaves can sell themselves or their children, numbers are induced to flock to great towns and cities, where many die from disappointed expectation, who would otherwise pick up a scanty subsistence in scattered villages.

6. Were slavery abolished, this evil could not happen: knowing they could not sell themselves or children, they would not be tempted to cities in such numbers; having only a precarious charity to rely on, they would substitute many modes of supplying a sustenance, from berries, herbs, &c.

7. It would appear to be the advantage of masters, to promote *the rearing of their slaves*. This, like many other theoretic ideas, is found to be fallacious, and contradicted by fact. The expense of rearing, and the loss incurred by the indispensable attendance of the parents on their offspring, has always made proprietors prefer *recruiting casual diminutions of their slaves by purchase*; even in Rome, where slavery was universal. How much more will masters avoid such trouble and expense in India, where I have seen, in a time of local scarcity only, a stout lad of fourteen or fifteen years old, sold for the trifling consideration of *two rupees*, scarcely a month's wages for the meanest servant.

7. Were voluntary servitude substituted for slavery, avarice could not affect population.

8. Women of bad fame purchase females for the most public prostitution, which are thereby lost to the community.

8. Abolish the unnatural law of slavery, and the evil could not occur.

9. Children are sometimes sold into bondage by the villany of others, in the case of death or absence of parents, instances of which are not uncommon.

9. Nor this.

10. The sanction of slavery, not many years ago, gave birth to an infamous traffic, and as injurious to our government as disgraceful to those concerned, diminishing our resources, by depriving us of subjects."

10. Nor this

"The effects of slavery are as plainly injurious, as the benefits of freedom are obvious and undoubted." *

* Par. Papers, pp. 301—303.

CHAP. II.

Nature and success of efforts for the abolition of the Slave Trade in India and the adjacent Islands—and the melioration of Slavery by the Hindoos, Mussulman, French, Dutch, and British.

The abolition of the Slave Trade, by the British nation, was attended with very salutary effects in British India. It is pleasing to trace the influence of just and humane principles in the abolition of the Slave Trade in our Eastern dominions; and the nature of the efforts, though partial, to meliorate the existing state of slavery in those extensive territories. For information respecting the present state of the Slave Trade, see Buxton's admirable work upon the subject.

Lord Cornwallis, Governor General of India, in a letter to the Court of Directors, in 1789, states his detestation of slavery, and his purpose to suppress it as far as he was able. —"An infamous traffic, it seems, has long been carried on in this country by the low Portuguese, and even by several foreign European seafaring people and traders, in purchasing and collecting native children in a clandestine manner, and exporting them for sale to the French Islands, and other parts of India. I have, at different times, taken steps to prevent the continuance of practices which are so shocking to humanity, and so pernicious to your interests. And, in order to deter all persons under the authority of this government, from being concerned in that species of trade, I lately directed that a commander of a country vessel, who carried off some children last winter, should be *prosecuted criminally* before the Supreme Court; and I have likewise published a proclamation, to give notice that any person living under the Company's protection, or in any shape under the authority of this government, who shall be convicted of carrying on, or aiding, or abetting the barbarous traffic that I have mentioned, will be certain of meeting with the most exemplary punishment. There are many obstacles in the way of abolishing slavery entirely in the Company's dominions, as the number of slaves is considerable, and the practice is sanctioned both by the Mahomedan and Hindoo laws. I have, however, a plan* under consideration, which I hope to be able to execute without doing much injury to the private interests, or offering

* "No further notice of the plan, here adverted to by his Lordship, has been traced upon the records of the Bengal Government."

great violence to the feelings of the natives, and which has for its object the abolition of the practice under certain limitations, and the establishing some regulations to alleviate, as much as may be possible, the misery of those unfortunate people during the time that they may be retained in that wretched situation."* A proclamation was made in the same year, and was "published in the English and country languages." Referring to the period at which it was issued, this document is of a very interesting character.†

It is pleasing at this period to see the French authorities in India co-operating with the British, in suppressing this trade in human beings. "We understand," says the *Calcutta Gazette*, in Sep. 1789, "Monsieur Montigny, Governor of *Chandernagore*, has lately issued a proclamation prohibiting all persons within the jurisdiction of the French Government, from purchasing or transporting any of the natives of these provinces as slaves; and, in order more effectually to prevent this infamous practice, a reward of *forty rupees* is offered to any person who shall give information of the offender, besides the sum of *ten rupees* to be given to each slave who shall be released in consequence. Both sums to be paid by the offender. The master attendant of *Chandernagore* is also directed to see that no native be embarked without an order signed by the Governor; and all captains of vessels trading to the port are strictly prohibited from receiving any natives on board. Nothing can reflect greater honour on the humanity of Monsieur Montigny, and the liberal policy of the French Government, than the above order; and we have no doubt this co-operation with the measures already taken by our own government, will put an effectual stop to this odious traffic."‡

Some free natives of Bengal having been taken to *St. Helena*, and sold as slaves, the practice was prohibited by authority. The Hon. Court of Directors, in a letter to the Governor General in 1793, observe—"It having been stated in the letter to you from the Governor and Council of St. Helena, in July, 1791, that they have heard of other complaints of the natives of Bengal, who were free, having been unjustly sold on that island, we direct that you cause an advertisement to be issued for the discovery thereof, and that you take the most effectual means for liberating such as may be under this unfortunate predicament; and for putting a stop to a practice so disgraceful to humanity, reporting your proceedings for our

* Par. Papers, 1828, p. 13. † p. 22.
‡ Par. Papers, pp. 18, 19. See also in 1791, pp. 34, 487, 493, 520.

information."* To secure the return of native servants, proceeding from Bengal to Europe, it was determined by the Government that a bond of 1,000 rupees should be given for each individual. "The humane purpose of this bond," says the Hon. Court, in 1796, "is sufficient to ensure our approbation of the measure."

The murder of a slave, under the Bengal Government, is made a capital offence. In 1799 was issued, "*A Regulation for certain modifications of the Mahomedan Law in cases of murder.*" It enjoins—"In every case of wilful murder, wherein the crime may appear to the court of Nizamut Adawlut to have been fully established against the prisoner, but the futwa of the law officers of that court shall declare the prisoner not liable under the Mahomedan law to suffer death by *kissans,* (or retaliation), solely on the ground of the prisoner's being father or mother, grandfather or grandmother, or other ancestor of the slain; or of the heirs of the slain, or one of the heirs of the slain, being the child, or grandchild, or other descendant of the prisoner; or of the slain having been the slave of the prisoner or of any other person, or a slave appropriated for the service of the public; or on any similar ground of personal distinction and exception from the general rules of equal justice; the court of Nizamut Adawlut, provided they see no circumstances in the case which may render the prisoner a proper object of mercy, shall sentence him to suffer death, as if the futwa of their law officers had declared him liable to *kissans,* or to suffer death by *seazut,* as authorised by the Mahomedan law in all cases of wilful murder, under the discretion vested in the Magistrate, with regard to this principle of punishment, for the ends of public justice."†

In 1796 a communication was addressed to the Governor of Bombay, from the Sultan and Chiefs of the island of *Johanna,* praying for assistance against the incursions of the French and Madagascar people, who destroyed and enslaved the inhabitants. They offer to "give these islands to the Company," and that "whatever shall be produced in this country, half shall be for you and the other half for us." In consideration of the friendly treatment which ships invariably received, at Johanna, some assistance was given to these islanders.‡ In 1813, an application was made to Bombay, by the Sultan of *Johanna,* respecting some persons who had been carried from the island to the *Mauritius* by the French, and there reduced

* Par. Papers, p. 45. † See p. 76.
‡ The letters are very interesting documents, pp. 82—84.

to slavery. The Hon. Court of Directors very humanely remark, upon the proceedings of the Indian Government,—"With respect to the circumstances alleged by the King of Johanna, of certain persons, his subjects, having been carried by the French to Mauritius, and there made slaves, we entirely approve of your suggestion to the Governor, for the purchase of such individuals, if in a state of slavery; and likewise of your further application, respecting several natives of our Indian provinces of both sexes, being in a state of slavery on that island, and requesting his assistance in obtaining their release, or in purchasing their freedom, and charging the expense to your Government." *

An important "*Regulation for preventing the importation of slaves from foreign countries, and the sale of slaves in the Territories immediately dependent on the Presidency of Fort William,*" was passed in 1811, by the Vice-President in Council. Copies of the regulation were ordered to be circulated among the officers of the *Bengal Government*, and also forwarded to those of *Fort St. George*, and *Bombay*. It was also resolved, that this "Regulation be sent to the political department, in order that a communication may be made to any of the *Native States*, which it may be deemed proper to apprize of the purport of the Regulation." †

The Resident at *Delhi*, in 1812, C. T. Metcalfe, Esq. (now Governor of Jamaica), actively prosecuted the humane measures of the Government. "The slave trade, which has been prohibited for a considerable time in the other provinces in the British dominions in India, continued to exist in the district of Delhi subsequently to its abolition in other places, no local orders having been issued for its discontinuance; and, in consequence, the resort of slave merchants to this quarter was becoming more frequent than ever. Being convinced, that it was not the intention of Government, that this iniquitous traffic should be encouraged in any part of its territories; satisfied rather that it was, and is, its earnest desire to abolish so abominable a commerce; I consider myself to be only fulfilling the manifest intentions of the Right Honorable the Governor-general in Council, *in putting a stop to the sale of human beings in the town and country of Delhi.* I have accordingly proclaimed the orders of Government for the abolition of the slave trade." ‡

The officers of the "*Nepaul* administration, in 1811 requested the co-operation of the British government, in their

* Par. Papers on Slavery in India, p. 224. † See p. 99. ‡ See p. 101.

measures towards an amelioration of the situation of the inhabitants of the mountains." The co-operation requested was cheerfully granted.*

"The regent at Gwalior, Baeja Bye, has been induced, from the representations of the British government, to abolish the traffic in slaves in her dominions. It appears that the traffic was open and avowed; that about *twenty slave dealers* resided in the bazaars of Gwalior, from which some idea may be formed of the extent of the trade. The Bye, it is said, will experience much difficulty in putting down *this trade of stealing children;* and it is only through the influence of the British government, that she will be able to overcome the opposition of interested Sirdars. The existence of slavery in the *Rajpoot states* contributes to the increase of crime in the British states, which are contiguous to them. It is essential to the good government of the Company's provinces, that the Slave Trade and slavery should be abolished in the Rajpoot and other territories of independent rajahs; and this we are happy to see is likely to be accomplished. The regent of Gwalior, the most powerful of the Mahratta states, has set the example, may it be speedily followed by the chiefs of all those states in which this practice has prevailed so long!"†

The following prohibition of slave dealing in *Oude*, is interesting.

PROCLAMATION ISSUED IN THE TERRITORIES OF OUDE.

Whereas repeated reports have reached our most blessed ears that slave-dealers, and after their example, sundry persons of other tribes, kidnapping male and female children, sell them; and whereas no practice can be more detestable than this, for it is nothing short of the destruction of human life; and whereas to our Majesty belongs the preservation of the people of God committed to our royal care, and *we do not permit injury to be done even to an ant, much less can our Majesty see unmoved the destruction of human beings!* It is, therefore, our royal wish that this horrible practice (of kidnapping) be at once eradicated from our royal dominions, and that this vile custom (of buying and selling human beings) be entirely and absolutely interdicted. We, therefore, command that henceforth no one, on any pretence or plea whatever, sell or buy human beings; and that the officers, both judicial and ministerial, of the capital and throughout our royal dominions, deem it imperative and incumbent on them to be ever watchful that this nefarious practice do not occur in any place; and that from those men whom they may suspect of having any connection or participation in this horrible practice, they require a penalty bond, and even sureties for good behaviour, otherwise to banish them from our royal territories. In this we command the officers aforesaid to be unremittingly vigilant; and if any one, after the issue of this mandate, be found guilty of this nefarious practice, he shall be apprehended, and an immediate report made of the circumstance to our exalted presence, that

* Par. Papers on Slavery in India, p. 115. See Par. Papers, 1838, p. 6.
† E. I. Mag. Feb. 1833, p. 203.

whatever punishment we are pleased to award in his behalf be forthwith carried into effect; and if there be any difficulty in the apprehension of such delinquents, that the same be reported to our exalted Majesty without loss of time, in order that the royal mandate may be issued without delay for their apprehension. Let this proclamation be promulged in all the alleys and streets, by the beat of drum, and copies of it, in the Persian and Hindee characters, be suspended in all the cutcherries, both civil and military, and in all public places of the resort of men, that *the sellers of human beings hereafter shall be sentenced to imprisonment for life in chains, and that the buyers shall likewise be most severely punished*; and that if any man clandestinely buy or sell God's people, the informant of such clandestine dealings shall receive a suitable reward; but if any one connive at such, he shall be punished accordingly.

Dated 7th Zeeqad, 1348, Hijree; corresponding
with 20th March, 1833.

The proceedings in India, are particularly worthy of notice, as it respects the bearing of the Act of Parliament, passed in the fifty-first year of his Majesty George III. commonly called the *Slave Felony Act*, or "*An Act for rendering more effectual an Act made in the forty-seventh year of his Majesty's reign, intituled, 'An Act for the Abolition of the Slave Trade.'*" Two hundred copies of this important act were printed in Calcutta, and duly circulated. A letter to the chief secretary at *Fort St. George*, and a similar one to *Bombay*, show the sense taken of this act in India. See this important communication at the foot of the page.*

* "The exact nature of the traffic in slaves, mentioned by you to be carried on from *Travancore*, not being stated in your letter, the Governor-general in council is of course precluded from forming a judgment, whether that traffic falls within the purview of the Act of the 51 Geo. III. c. 23, intituled, "An Act for rendering more effectual an Act made in the forty-seventh year of his Majesty's reign, intituled, 'An Act for the Abolition of the Slave Trade.'" With respect to that particular point, his lordship in council can only observe, that *he does not consider the provisions of the Act in question, applicable to the importation or removal of slaves by land.* It having been deemed proper, to consider maturely the measures which should be pursued by the local governments of this country, with respect to the above mentioned statute, the following is the purport of the resolutions adopted by the Governor-general in council on that subject.

"The provisions of the Act being highly penal in their operation, and its object very important, the Governor-general in council has considered it proper to order a copy of it to be published in the *Calcutta Gazette*, for general information. In like manner, his lordship in council has directed copies of the Act to be forwarded to the local governments of *Bombay, Java*, of *Prince of Wales' Island, Mauritius, Ceylon*, and *the residents at the Moluccas*, and *Fort Marlborough*. On the same principle, copies of the statute will be forwarded to the magistrates of *Chittagong* and *Cuttack*, in order that in their capacity of justices of the peace, under the law of England, they may aid in enforcing the provisions of the statute.

"The Governor in Council, at Fort St. George, is aware that a Regulation was some time ago passed at this Presidency, for preventing the importation of slaves from foreign countries. Inquiries will be made, with the view of ascertaining whether the provisions of that regulation have been effectual in preventing that species of traffic; if not, a further regulation will be passed without loss

The Bombay Government, in 1813, issued a "*Regulation for preventing the importation of slaves from foreign countries, and the sale of such slaves, in the territories immediately dependent on the Presidency of Bombay.*"* A difference of opinion upon the application of this act to India has been entertained; that of the Advocate-General of Bombay, H. G. Macklin, Esq., is expressed in the following terms, in a letter to the Secretary to Government:—

"With great deference to the opinion of the right honourable the Governor-general in council, I think the act extends *to importation by land as well as sea.* In the preamble it is recited, that it is fit such measures should be extended, to the effectual abolition of the slave trade wheresoever it may be attempted to practise the same; and, in the enacting part immediately following,—'If any person residing or being in any of the islands, &c., or territories under the government of the United Company of Merchants trading to the East Indies, shall carry away or remove, as a slave or slaves, &c., any person or persons whatsoever from any part of *Africa*, or from any other country, territory, or place whatsoever; or shall import or bring, &c., into any island, colony, country, territory, or place whatsoever, any such persons as aforesaid, for the purpose aforesaid: then in every such case, the persons so offending, are declared to be felons.' This enactment is taken verbatim from the statute, and appears to me, to comprehend every possible case of the importation of slaves into British territories. The act is highly penal, and I have great satisfaction in observing that his lordship in council is resolved to lay before the hon. court the difficulties which attend carrying the penal part of the statute into execution in India, where slavery is of a much milder feature than in the western hemisphere. The manumission of the slave will be sufficiently provided for by the regulation, and the King's courts may act upon the statute in cases of aggravation or enormity."†

A proclamation against the Slave-trade was issued by the Government in Madras, in 1790, similar to the one issued by the Marquis Cornwallis, in 1789.‡

It is grateful to see the *Dutch* authorities in India, at this period, co-operating with the British, in suppressing the detestable traffic in human beings. The following letter was addressed to the Governor of Madras, in 1793:—"Favoured

of time, establishing severer penalties for the infringement of the prohibition now existing under the regulation above noticed, of the importation of slaves from foreign countries, in conformity to the spirit of the statute, to which the foregoing remarks allude. These remarks, it is presumed, will inform the Governor in council sufficiently of the construction annexed by the Governor-general in council to the Act of the 51 Geo. III. c. 23, and of the measures which it has been judged necessary to adopt at this Presidency. It is scarcely necessary to add, that his lordship in council is of opinion that similar measures should be adopted by the government of Fort St. George, with such modifications as local circumstances may suggest, without of course departing from the principle on which the measures above detailed are founded.

I have, &c.

G. Dowdeswell, Sec. to Government Judicial Department.

Fort William, Sept. 26th, 1812.§

* Par. Papers, p. 216. † pp. 216, 217. ‡ pp. 469, 470. § p. 137.

with your honour's letter, we cannot indeed emphatically enough express our indignation and aversion with regard to so horrible an event, as the exportation of 180 natives from *Bimlipatam,* as slaves, in a French brigantine bound to the French islands; which, however, according to the declaration that came enclosed, was surprised and taken at Pedir by the Malays, who killed all those that were on board of her, and did not escape out of their hands. To show how much the exportation of the unhappy creatures merits our disgrace, we shall renew, in the strongest manner, our orders to our northern factories, to oppose such inhuman practice; not only by our subjects, but also with all possible diligence by strangers, in case they should think our territory a safe place for it; with a charge to deliver the unhappy creatures out of the hands of those who will not desist, but are refractory, either by good or forcible means, and to send them to one of your agents for the protection of their liberty, and for their support. We feel the propriety of your honour's resolution, that such kidnapping may be prevented, to check it with exemplary punishment; and, in case any of our subjects transgress the orders instituted against it, they shall be seized and delivered over to justice, to be punished according to the exigency of the case."*

In 1819, some vigorous steps were taken by the *Dutch* to abolish slavery in *Malacca.* The following document, signed by more than *seventy* of the principal inhabitants, is very interesting:—"List of the inhabitants of *Malacca,* who after a speech by the Governor (Dec. 1819), in which he inspired and recommended them to acts of humanity, have bound themselves, this day, as a token of their joy, for the memorable birth-day of their beloved and honoured hereditary Prince of the *Netherlands,* to acknowledge that no children of their slaves, that may be born from and after this date, shall be considered as slaves, but as free born children; and as the parents are slaves, and have not the means to provide for their education, they shall remain with their parents, and be under the immediate care of the master or mistress of their parents, until they shall have attained the age of *sixteen* years."†

These extracts show the efforts of the European authorities in India, with the occasional co-operation of the natives, to abolish the slave trade. The success experienced in these

* Par. Papers, pp. 537, 538. See Par. Papers, 1838, p. 244—247.
† Par Papers, 1838, p. 248.

humane efforts should have encouraged them to attempt more than has yet been done;—*not merely to meliorate, but to abolish slavery in the East*. In consequence of the active measures described, many slaves have been liberated, and their importation into India, by sea, in a great degree prohibited.

It is interesting to trace *the melioration of slavery in the East*. From the following extract of a translation of the Hindoo Laws, transmitted by the Bengal Government to the Hon. Court of Directors in 1774, it appears that the Hindoos admit various modes of enfranchising slaves.—

"Whoever is born of a female slave; whoever hath been purchased for a price; whoever hath been found by chance anywhere; and whoever is a slave by descent from his ancestors:—these four species of slaves, until they are freed by the voluntary consent of their master, cannot have their liberty. If their master, from a principle of beneficence, gives them liberty, they become free.

"Whoever, having received his victuals from a person during the time of a famine, hath become his slave, *upon giving to his provider whatever he received from him during the time of famine, and also two head of cattle, may become free from his servitude*; according to the ordinations of *Pachesputtee Misr*, approved. Chendeesur, speaks thus: That he who has received victuals during a famine, and hath, by those means, become a slave, on giving *two head of cattle to his provider, may become free*.

"Whoever, having been given up as a pledge for money lent, performs service to the creditor, recovers his liberty whenever the debtor discharges the debt. If the debtor neglects to pay the creditor his money, and takes no thought of the person whom he left as a pledge, that person becomes the purchased slave of the creditor.

"Whoever being unable to pay his creditor a debt, hath borrowed a sum of money from another person, and paid his former creditor, and hath thus become a slave to the second creditor; or who, to silence the importunities of his creditor's demands, hath yielded himself a slave to that creditor, such kind of slaves shall not be released from servitude until payment of the debts.

"Whoever, by the loss of chance in any game, and by the fortune of war is enslaved, these persons, *upon giving two others in exchange, are released from their servitude!*

"If the slave of one person 'goes to another, and of his own desire consents to be the slave of that person, in this case he must still be the property of the person to whom he was first a slave. The mode of release for every kind of slave shall take place according to the ordination laid down for each.

"A *Chehtree* and *Bice*, who, after having been *Sinasses* (religious mendicants) apostate from that way of life, and are become the slaves of the magistrate, can never be released.

"If a Brahmin hath committed this crime, the magistrate shall not make him a slave; but, *having branded him in the forehead with the print of a dog's foot, shall banish him the kingdom*.

"Whoever hath yielded himself a slave for a stipulated time, upon the completion of that term, shall recover his freedom.

"Whoever performs a servitude for his subsistence, shall recover his freedom upon renouncing that subsistence.

"Whoever, for the sake of a slave girl, becomes a slave to any person, he shall recover his freedom upon renouncing the slave girl.

"Whoever hath become a slave by selling himself to any person, he shall not be free until the master, of his own accord, gives him his freedom.

"If the master, from a principle of beneficence, give him his liberty, he becomes free.

"If a thief, having stolen the child of any person, sells it to another, or a man, by absolute violence, forces another to be a slave, *the magistrate shall restore such person to his freedom.*

"If the master of a slave should be in imminent danger of his life, and this slave, by his own efforts and presence of mind, is able to save the life of his master, *the slave shall be freed from his servitude, and be held as a son.* If he choose, he may stay with his master, or quit that place, and go where he will be at liberty.

"Whoever is without a legitimate child, and hath a child from the womb of a slave girl, *she, together with her son, becomes free.*

"When any person, from a principle of beneficence, would release his slave, this is the mode: the slave shall fill a pitcher with water, and put therein *berenge-a-rook* (rice that has been cleansed without boiling), and *flowers and doub* (a kind of small salad), and, taking the pitcher upon his shoulder, shall stand near his master; and the master putting the pitcher upon the slave's head, shall break the pitcher, so that the water, rice, flowers, and doub, that were in the pitcher, may fall upon the slave's body; after that, the master shall three times pronounce the words, '*I have made you free.*' The slave shall take some steps towards the east, and he shall be free.

"Whoever hath become a slave to any person, *the master is proprietor of any property which that slave may acquire, exclusive of the price of his own slavery, and exclusive also of any thing which may be given to him as a present.*"*

"I make no scruple," says Sir W. Jones, in his charge to the Grand Jury at Calcutta, in 1785, to "declare my own opinion, that absolute unconditional slavery, by which one human creature becomes the property of another, like a horse or an ox, is happily unknown to the laws of England, and that no human law could give it a just sanction; yet, though I hate the word, the continuance of it, properly explained, can produce little mischief. I consider slaves as servants under a contract, expressed or implied, and made either by themselves or by such persons as are authorised by nature or law to contract for them, until they attain a due age to cancel or confirm any compact that may be disadvantageous to them. I have slaves whom I rescued from death or misery, but consider them as other servants, and shall certainly tell them so, when they are old enough to comprehend the difference of the terms."†

In the province of *Dacca* many children were kidnapped, given away, or sold by their parents into slavery; a number of these were recovered, and restored to their parents or relations. The collector of Dacca, in 1787, addressed the Superintendents of Police at Calcutta—"I have the pleasure to acknowledge the receipt of your letter, accompany-

* Par. Papers on Slavery in India, 1828, pp. 7, 8. † pp. 9, 10, and 710.

ing *twelve* boys and *twenty-one* girls belonging to this district, under charge of Churreemeulah and three other peons, and which, in obedience to the wish of the Right Honourable the Governor-general, shall be restored to their parents or relations, in the same manner as those transmitted to me two years since."*

It appears to be a received opinion among the Mahomedans, that murder may be atoned for by money, or by giving a slave. In 1790 two persons, named Mungaly Khan, and Assud Khan, were convicted of the murder of Nowaz Khan, and were ordered to make a pecuniary compensation to the plaintiffs, viz., Peranow the widow, and the brothers of the deceased. In conformity with the Nawaub's orders, they were called upon to pay "*the price of blood.*" The widow stated, "Mungaly Khan being unable to pay a pecuniary compensation, has *given to me his son, to be my servant for life.* Assud Khan has given me, in satisfaction of the murder, his share of the village of Caympoor." The other plaintiffs declaring, "In consequence of the poverty and distress of Mungaly Khan and Assud Khan, they remitted their claim to a compensation." The Governor-general, Earl Cornwallis, and his council, disapproved of the proceeding, agreeing that—"The Naib Nazim be recommended not to admit of Mungaly Khan's making over his son as a slave for life to Peranow, and that he be requested to levy the amount of the compensation, which it may be determined to exact from Mungaly Khan, by the customary mode of process."†

Ceylon has been a market of slaves from *Bengal.* In 1789, a "Captain Horrebow took on board at Fultah, 150 children, whom, previously to his departure, he purchased in Bengal: he transported them, under English colours, to Columbo, where they were sold as slaves. The Dutch Governor, Mynheer Van De Grave, in terms most honourable to himself, refused to permit their being landed: but Captain Horrebow found means to elude the vigilance of the Governor, and availed himself of an excellent market for his wares."‡ He "was sentenced to be imprisoned for three months, to pay a fine of 500 rupees, and to give security for his future good behaviour for three years; himself in a bond of 10,000 rupees, and two sureties in 5,000 rupees each."§

* Par. Papers, 1828, p. 12. † p. 27. ‡ p. 14. § p. 21.

The state of slavery in *Ceylon*, previously to its subjugation by the British, and the mitigation of it proposed by the conquering power, are ably stated in a communication to the Marquis Wellesley, Governor-general of India, in 1800. A short extract only is given :—

"The manner in which the unhappy persons, whom it is the principal object of the proposed regulations to protect, are treated in general by their masters and mistresses of every nation, cast, and religion, within these settlements, render it a positive duty of Government, to delay, as little as possible, the adoption of strong measures for their relief. Those which I propose are taken chiefly from the statutes of Batavia, particularly from one published in the year 1770, and which was in force at the time of our occupation of this island. I have also recurred, in some instances to the civil law, on which the jurisprudence of Holland is founded; and, as the principal class of the proprietors of slaves are of the Mahomedan religion, I have adopted, and made general some of the regulations by which the *Khoran* and its commentators have softened the rigours of slavery, at the same time that they established its lawfulness. The principal point on which all codes which have allowed domestic slavery have universally insisted, *the clear and unequivocal definition of the slave, and of the means by which he or she may have been acquired*, was neglected in Ceylon with the most barbarous indifference. Of more than a hundred cases that have been brought before me, the masters or mistresses of the beings claiming liberty, have not, in more than six or seven instances, produced slave bonds properly authenticated. In many cases no papers are existing; in others simple testamentary devises, proving the opinion of the defunct as to his power over the slave bequeathed, have been insisted on, not as a collateral, but as a positive proof of the slavery of the person claimed. In the province of Baticalva, the assertion that a child was sold by his parents in a famine, was urged before me, as the right on which the greater part of the slaves in that province have been held for some time past, as well as their posterity. The practice of kidnapping at *Cochin*, was, for many years, notorious; but the reception of slaves from that place was subject to scarcely any restrictions on this island; and those restrictions, I am afraid, were but ill observed. *That institution, reprobated as it is by good policy, morality, and religion, exists here with all the aggravated horrors of uncertainty in its application, and cruelty in its exercise.*"*

The *abolition of slavery in Ceylon* is thus described by Sir A. Johnstone, in a letter to the late Sir W. W. Wynn, Esq. :— "As the right of every proprietor of slaves to continue to hold slaves in Ceylon was guaranteed to him, by the capitulation under which the Dutch possession had been surrendered to the British arms, in 1794, the British Government of Ceylon conceived that, however desirable the measure might be, they had not a right to abolish slavery in Ceylon by any legislative act. A proposition was made on the part of Government by me, to the proprietors of the slaves in 1806, before trial by jury was introduced, urging them to adopt some plan of their own accord for the gradual abolition of slavery: this proposition, at that time, they unanimously rejected. The right of sitting upon juries was granted to the

* Par. Papers, 1828, pp. 84—92.

inhabitants of Ceylon in 1811. From that period I availed myself of the opportunities which were afforded to me, when I delivered my charge at the commencement of each session to the jurymen—most of whom were considerable proprietors of slaves—of informing them what was doing in England upon the subject of the abolition of slavery, and of pointing out to them the difficulties which they themselves must frequently experience, in executing, with impartiality, their duties as jurymen, in all cases in which slaves were concerned. A change of opinion upon the subject of slavery was gradually perceptible among them; and, in the year 1816, the proprietors of slaves, of all casts and religious persuasions in Ceylon, sent me their unanimous resolutions, to be publicly recorded in court, declaring *free all children born of their slaves from the 12th of August*, 1816. This, in the course of a few years, must put an end to the state of slavery which had existed in Ceylon for more than three centuries."*

Appended to the Par. Papers on Slavery in India, of 1838, is a collection of papers relative to slavery in Ceylon, moved for by W. Evans, Esq., M. P. They contain a very full and interesting account of the movement in 1816, to declare all slaves born after the birth-day of the Prince Regent, free. The unanimity of this measure is very striking, and augurs well. *The Kandian provinces in the interior were not included in this measure.* The slave population in 1829 was 2,113. The reply of the chiefs relative to the time of emancipation is very characteristic—"We most earnestly pray, that, in consideration of our fidelity and attachment to government, this gracious government will also have compassion towards us, and refrain from liberating the female slaves for these *sixty years*, so that for a *short space* of time we may continue free from inconvenience; and that it may be so regulated, that female slaves born after the lapse of these sixty years shall be paid for at the rate of 100 ridies for each, (£3 6s. 8d.) and thus a gradual emancipation of female slaves be effected thenceforward as his Excellency had suggested."—Dec. 1831. The Governor, in reply, states his intention of "visiting Kandy, for the purpose of personally entering upon this very important question; and he cannot but hope that, on more mature consideration, they will be

* Ori. Herald, vol. xvi. p. 136. "At a levee of Cingalese Chiefs, held at *Kandy*, Jan. 1832, the Governor, Sir W. Horton, declared it to be the intention of Government gradually to abolish slavery throughout the Island, and called upon the Chiefs to afford their assistance in this benevolent work."—E. I. Mag., Sep. 1832, p. 291.

inclined to make arrangements for *more speedily* carrying into effect a measure so highly creditable to themselves, and so much in unison with the wishes of his Majesty's Government."* The latest intelligence upon the subject is contained in despatches from the Right Hon. Lord Glenelg, under date Oct. 1827, and April, 1838. No information can be gathered of the time determined for the abolition of slavery in Kandy. Sir Alexander Johnstone suggested to the British Government the propriety of erecting "a monument in Colombo, with the names inscribed on it of all the proprietors of domestic slaves who signed the resolution of August 12, 1816, and thereby to commemorate the event in a manner flattering to the feelings of all the natives of Asia."† The names of the proprietors amounted to 763. It is to be deeply regretted that this suggestion was not adopted, on the ground that "the length of time which has elapsed rendered it unnecessary and inexpedient." It is presumed very few will cherish the same opinion, but rather desire that such a monument of the triumphs of our common humanity may grace the beautiful island of Ceylon. May every slave community merit such a trophy, and enjoy its exhibition!

The valuable co-operation of the Rajah of *Kotah* with the Resident at *Delhi,* in 1808, in the suppression of the *sale of children into slavery,* shows how much Europeans in India may accomplish for the interests of humanity.‡ In 1836, his Highness, the Rao of *Cutch,* issued a proclamation for the suppression of the slave-trade.§

While the *Island of Java* continued in the possession of the British, the abolition of the slave-trade, and the improvement of the condition of the slaves, was considered an object of importance. The importation of slaves into the island, after the commencement of 1813, was prohibited by proclamation; and instructions on the subject were sent to "the islands depending on the Government."‖ Previously to the transfer of Java to the Dutch, the slaves were emancipated. Upon which the Hon. Court of Directors declared,—"We entirely approve of your proceedings, in emancipating the slaves at Java, previously to the transfer of that place to the Dutch, as we do of the option you gave to all the slaves, of being conveyed, at the public charge, to their native country."¶

The slave-trade appears to have been very effectually sup-

* Par. Papers, 1838, p. 611. † Par. Papers, 1838, p. 614.
‡ Par. Papers, pp. 99, 100. See also Par. Papers, 1838, p. 5.
§ Par. Papers, 1838, p. 151.
‖ Par. Papers, p. 185; see also pp. 168, 169. ¶ p. 265.

pressed under the Bengal Government, by the humane and vigorous efforts above described. The magistrates of the *Bareilly* Court, in 1812, state—"We have now the honour to submit attested copies of the answers received from *eight* out of the *nine* magistrates under our authority; from which it will be evident to Government that, since the promulgation of the regulation above specified, the traffic in slaves imported from foreign countries is almost, if not entirely, suppressed in the districts of *Bareilly, Moradabad, Cawnpoor, Furruckabad, Etawah, Agra, Alligurh, and Seharunpore South.*"* "But, it should be understood, *the slave-owners still disposed of those who were actually slaves, as part of their real property.*"†

The British Government in India has abolished *the duty levied on the sale of slaves,* by the former Government of *Kumaon,* and suppressed the traffic in slaves in those countries bordering on *Nepaul,* which were brought under its authority by treaty in 1815. This duty or tax was, for every male and female slave, *two rupees eight annas.* "We cannot touch on this subject," said the late Marquis of Hastings, "without adverting to a consequence of our having wrested the hill country from the Ghorkas, in which your Hon. Court will feel the most lively satisfaction. A slave-trade of great extent has been totally extinguished; and the hapless families, from whom the Ghorkas used to tear away the children for sale, have now to look with joyful confidence on the security bestowed towards their offspring by the British Government."‡

In this part of India, an extraordinary practice existed, of *selling wives and widows,* which has been abolished.§ The Governor-general, in 1826, wrote to the Court of Directors—"We took measures to furnish the Commissioner, without delay, with the form of proclamation approved by us, prohibiting the *sale of wives and widows by their husbands or late husband's family.* We need not repeat the expression of our determination to put down so barbarous and hateful a custom."‖

The *Calcutta Journal,* in March, 1824, contained an article

* Par. Papers, p. 140. † p. 141. ‡ p. 266. See Heber's Jour. vol. i. p. 492.

§ "The people of *Laos* are in great dread of the *Burmese,* and the cruel system of border warfare and man-catching, to which our occupation of the Tenasserim provinces has put an end to the southward, still continues in force to the north, between *Laos* and *Ava.* It would appear that, as in Burmah, women are bought and sold at Laos. The price of one is ten head of cattle, or twenty-five rupees."—*Asi. Jour.*, Nov. 1830, p. 256.

‖ Par. Papers, 1828, p. 416; and Par. Papers, 1838, p. 360.

entitled, the "*Slave-Trade in British India.*" A brief extract only is given:—

"Our readers are of course aware, that the nefarious traffic in human beings is equally forbidden by the letter and the spirit of British law in every portion of the British dominions, be their geographical position what it may, whether in the frozen regions of the north, or the scorching climate of the torrid zone; wherever the British flag waves, the disgraceful commerce is made criminal by British law; what then will the humane and enlightened community of this magnificent capital of our eastern possessions say, when they are told, that with all its glittering spires of the temples of a pure religion—all its splendid palaces, bespeaking the taste, the refinement, and the riches of their inhabitants—with all its colleges, and schools, and societies, to promote the propagation of knowledge, civil and religious;—what will they say, when they learn that, amidst all these signs of veneration for Christianity, the philanthropy, the greatness, and the refinement of Britons and British subjects, in a British capital, it is disgraced by witnessing the lowest degradation of the human species?—*that this great capital is, in short, at once the depôt of the commerce and riches of the east, and the mart in which the manacled African is sold, like the beast of the field, to the highest bidder.* It is known, too, that the Arab ships are in the habit of carrying away many of the natives of this country, principally females, and disposing of them in Arabia, in barter for African slaves for the Calcutta market! Can it be possible that such degrading, such wicked scenes are passing around us, and that the actors are suffered to escape unnoticed and unpunished? We fear the fact is too true; but we hope that the publicity thus given to it will lead to the prevention of such gross violations of law and humanity in future. We can conceive the difficulty of detection in these cases; but let all those who are aware of the illicit practices of these followers of Mahomed, remember that they are imperiously called on as Christians, and as British subjects in particular, to bring to punishment these violators of law and humanity. Nature shudders at the thought of the barbarities practised by these abusers of God's noblest creatures, who are led by an accursed thirst of gold to brutalize the human species."* For the secret prevalence of slavery in Calcutta, see *E. I. Mag.*, June, 1838, pp. 552—564.

The magistrates of Calcutta immediately addressed the Government upon the subject, acknowledging,—"Under the provision of Reg. X., 1811, a bond is taken from the commanders of a certain class of ships, previously to their being allowed to land their cargoes; and they are also required to give in a list of their crews and passengers. We must confess, however, that these are *very inadequate restrictions* to prevent the introduction of slaves into the town; the penalty could only be enforced by the detection of the offence, which is attended with much difficulty."† Translations in the Persian and Arabic languages were made of an extract of the 51 Geo. III. c. 23,‡ for circulation among the merchants; which measure was certainly of a decisive character.

* Par. Papers on Slavery in India, p. 378; and P. Papers, 1838, p. 307.

† p. 377.

‡ Par. Papers, p. 380. By a more recent act of Parliament, 4 Geo. IV. c. 27, the traffic in slaves has been declared to be an act of piracy, and all British subjects who may be concerned in it, are liable to be dealt with accordingly.

Slaves appear still to be clandestinely imported into India. A Calcutta paper, in 1830, contains the following extract from a native paper:—"'Jewellery, and other articles, to the value of *four lacks of rupees*, had been offered by a European jeweller for purchase by the king (of *Oude*), who took other merchandise in the shape of a batch of newly-imported *Abyssinians*, which had been offered for sale, and bought by his Majesty.' This demands, and we hope will receive investigation; and if it is properly conducted, and all the obstacles to the prosecution of the offenders are removed, we venture to predict that it will be found that the importation of slaves continues to be carried on, to an extent utterly disgraceful."*

The opinion of the recorder of *Prince of Wales Island* was taken in 1821—"as to the legality of apprehending and sending back to Malacca a runaway slave." This important question was answered in a Letter to the Secretary of Government. "I have the honour to acknowledge the receipt of yours, with a copy of a dispatch from the Governor of Malacca. I am not acquainted with the Dutch language; and, therefore, if there should be any circumstance in that part of the dispatch which varies the question submitted to me, from the letter of the Governor of Malacca in French, I should wish to have a translation of it; but, as it is not probable, I do not delay my request, that you will communicate to the Honourable the Governor in Council, that in the absence of any treaty, *I am of opinion, that the slave in question cannot be legally secured and sent back to Malacca.*"†

A number of slaves, procured in the vicinity of *Juggernaut's Temple in Orissa*, 1790, were liberated, and the captain of the vessel severely reprimanded, and threatened that, "on committing a second offence, he should be punished to the utmost rigour of the law, and sent by the first conveyance to England."‡ Some slaves from *Ganjam* were also set at liberty, and the slave-trader directed to be "fined the sum of 200 rupees (to be distributed amongst the natives liberated from the vessel under his command), imprisoned for three months, until he pays the fine, and that he be then publicly expelled the district."§

The sale of slaves, under the Madras Government, for the arrears of the State, was not discontinued till 1819. The Secretary writes to the Collector of *Malabar*:—"The Board's

* India Gaz., June, 1830. Asi. Jour. Dec. 1830, p. 191. See Asi. Jour., March, 1831, p. 123. See also Par. Papers, 1838, p. 6.

† Par. Papers on Slavery in India, p. 462; see also p. 456.

‡ p. 476. § p. 494.

proceedings on the general subject of slavery have been laid before the Government, whose final orders will hereafter be communicated to you; but, in the mean time, I am directed to desire, that *the practice of selling slaves for arrears of revenue, may be immediately discontinued.*"* Slaves on the government lands of *Malabar* have been liberated, Nov. 1837.†

Some successful measures are in prosecution to abolish slavery in *Arracan.* "When Arracan was under the Burman dominion, the inhabitants were allowed to have both permanent and temporary slaves. Since the English took possession of the province, the system of permanent slavery has been entirely prohibited by the Government."—*E. I. Mag.*, 1834, p. 461—463. *Assam* is also receiving the ameliorating influence of our connexion. The population of Durung, one of its districts, affords some data on which to ascertain the prevalence of slavery:

Free persons	86,041
Slaves	2,301
Bondmen	1,177
	89,519

The entire number of slaves in Assam is estimated at 11,300, and of bondmen, 5,784. The draft of a regulation for the abolition of slavery in this province has been circulated among the public authorities. It may be anticipated that this new territory may be speedily blessed with the suppression of slavery.‡

A communication from the authorities of Bombay to the Hon. Court of Directors, under date March, 1837, is very interesting. Reference is made "to the existence of a considerable trade in slaves, between the dominions of the Imam of *Muscat,* the coasts of *Arabia,* and the ports of *Cutch* and *Kattywar,* and to the measures suggested for its suppression. Your Hon. Court will perceive, that the whole of the chiefs who possess ports in Kattywar have readily consented to assist in the suppression of the slave-trade, with the exception of the Nawaub of Joonaghey, whose answer had not been received." It is added, "any danger lest this precedent of forbearance should be abused in the manner pointed out by the Advocate-general, in his letter of Jan. 1836, must be obviated by giving strong and explicit warning throughout the eastern seas, that no indulgence is to be expected by slave-traders in future."§

* Par. Papers on Slavery in India, p. 873. † Par. Papers, 1838, p. 35.
‡ See E. I. Mag. Jan. 1837, pp. 41—45. § Par. Papers, 1838, pp. 15—19.

It is pleasing to observe some progress made in the suppression of the slave-trade, and even of slavery itself. Of *Coorg* it is stated, in Nov. 1836—"We learned with much satisfaction *the emancipation of the whole of the Punnah slaves in Coorg*, and considered the manner in which Captain Le Hardy proceeded to carry into effect the orders of Government very creditable to that officer."* It is highly gratifying to find that our possession of the *Tenasserim* provinces on the coast has been indirectly the cause of a great benefit to the people of the interior, by means of a great falling off in the trade in slaves, which in these countries appears to have been attended with circumstances of even unusual atrocity.†

Under the Kandyan Government (in Ceylon,) there were a number of slaves attached to the royal household, but they were emancipated by the British soon after the accession.‡

"It has been universally taught by example, that British law regards the life of a slave as of the same value as the life of a Brahmin: that in the courts of justice his person will receive the same protection, and his word the same weight. His ill-treatment is an especial object of inquiry to the magistrate. These vital and important changes, some legal and proclaimed, others moral and silent, have obliterated the brand set upon him as an outcast of society, and have paved the way, as far as legal enactments can effect the purpose, towards the further annihilation of the social distinctions which still mark him."§

These extracts display the humane and vigorous efforts of the British functionaries in India to abolish the slave-trade, and mitigate the evils of slavery. The state of slavery at the present period next demands attention. The following chapter will show that much remains to be done, before every British subject in India is free.

CHAP. III.

The present state and extent of Slavery in British India—Probable number of slaves—Want of more correct information.

The nature and extent of slavery in the British territories in India, is a subject that cannot but be deeply interesting to

* Par. Papers on Slavery in India, 1838, p. 9. † p. 10. ‡ p. 608. § p. 419.

every liberal and humane mind. The following extracts from the Par. Papers on East India Slavery, will throw some light on a subject upon which little correct information is possessed.

The Resident at Delhi, in 1812, C. T. Metcalfe, Esq., issued a proclamation *prohibiting the sale of slaves.* On this subject the Governor-general addressed the Court of Directors, in 1813:—"We observed, that the proclamation not only prohibited the importation of slaves for sale into the assigned territories, but the sale of slaves *actually within those territories* previously to its promulgation; *a meusure which we were not prepared to sanction.* Odious and abominable as such a traffic is, although it must be admitted that the system of slavery in this country is infinitely mitigated, when compared with that against which the enactments of the legislature in England have been directed. *The laws, which have hitherto been enacted to restrain it, have been confined in their object to* THE TRADE IN SLAVES BY IMPORTATION OR EXPORTATION; *but they have not been extended to the emancipation of persons already in a state of slavery, nor to the prohibition of their transfer, by sale, to other masters, within the country which they inhabit.*"*

But, though the sale of slaves was thus prohibited in the province of Delhi, slavery is still continued. This is evident from the Resident's communication to Government:—"In issuing a proclamation for the abolition of the future importation and sale of slaves, I had no idea of infringing on the rights of the actual proprietors of slaves. *The proprietors of slaves in this territory, notwithstanding that proclamation, retain all their rights over their slaves, except that of selling them or making them the property of another.* This is perfectly understood, in consequence of the decisions given in the court of judicature in trials between owners and slaves. I have more than once embraced the opportunity afforded by such trials, to explain publicly, that *slaves are still the property of their owners,* though not disposable property."†

The magistrate of *Bareilly* in 1812, referring to the efficacy of the provisions of Regulation X., 1811, for preventing the importation of slaves from foreign countries, remarks, "This traffic, I believe, has suffered a very material check since the promulgation of the Regulation, inasmuch as children are no longer brought down from the hills, and publicly exposed for

* Par. Papers on Slavery in India, pp. 101, 102; see also p. 134.
† p. 104.

sale, as formerly, within this district; but, *children are still sold within the Company's provinces, by subjects of the British Government, nor does the Regulation contain any prohibition of such sale!* Parents, prevented by poverty from rearing a large family, will dispose of their children to an advantage, when offered, rather than allow them to starve; the feelings of nature will confine this traffic to cases of necessity only, and will act more forcibly than any legal prohibition in preventing abuses; it may be much doubted, indeed, whether the condition of children imported from the hills was not, in most cases, much ameliorated by such importation."*

The Rev. J. Fern, late missionary in *Travancore*, gives an affecting account of the slaves. "They present a wretched appearance to the beholder. There is a custom of giving them a cloth occasionally, the only clothing they wear. I am not aware of any provision for age or sickness. Slaves are out of society, out of caste, except as between themselves. They live together in the fields and out-parts, adjacent upon the villages: they are frequently transferred. The price of a good slave is about 300 pence. I suppose they are seizable for the debts of their masters. I know of no restriction. Husbands and wives are separated, by sale, to different parties! whether it is of frequent occurrence I do not know. The slaves are in the lowest possible state of degradation: if it were lawful so to speak of fellow-creatures possessing the same capabilities, I would say that they were wild men. Nothing but Christianity descends or can descend low enough to meet them, and to raise them to the level of mankind. The bible is the only book adapted to them in their present state."†

A Mr. Browne, the proprietor of an estate at *Anjarakandy*, in *Malabar*, claimed *the right of a master over some slaves*, as a part of the Mahomedan law, under which he considered the provinces of the Madras Presidency to be governed. "I cannot (says the Chief Secretary of the Government in 1813) agree to the proposition, that these provinces are, so far as relates to *British subjects*, governed by the Mahomedan law. In questions of civil right, they are governed by the laws of the different nations to whom justice is to be dispensed. In criminal prosecutions, the Mahomedan law is (for what reason I do not know,) established over all the natives in the Provinces, but not over the British. They retain the rights of their birth, and ought also to retain all the relations con-

* Par. Papers on Slavery in India, p. 141.

† Par Papers, 1832, p. 550.

nected with the British character, *to which it is equally abhorrent to be the master of slaves, as to endure slavery.* It is expressly provided, in the several statutes, that our law shall not interfere with the authority exercised by the heads of families amongst the natives; who, from local residence at the Presidencies, are made subject in general to the British laws, but *no such provision is made for British subjects as the masters of slaves!*"

The Advocate-general expressed the same opinion; and this important position, that *a Briton in India cannot be a slave-holder,* was thus definitely determined by a letter from the Chief Secretary to the Government, Fort William, in 1813, to the Secretary of the Madras Government:—"The Advocate-general, having stated it as his opinion that it is quite impracticable, as the law at present stands, for *any British subject, to support a claim to the person or services of any one residing within the limits of the British territories as a slave;* and that opinion corresponding entirely with the sentiments entertained by the Right Honorable the Governor-general in Council on the subject, his Lordship in Council thinks that every case of that nature which may be brought before the Governor in Council of Fort St. George, should be regarded as an illegal and unauthorized assumption of power; and that legal measures should be resorted to, should circumstances appear to require it, against any British subject so acting in violation of the law."* The difference between the state of public opinion, feeling, and, we may add, law, in the East and in the West Indies, previously to the abolition of negro slavery, cannot fail to strike the attention of every reader. It is very justly observed, "the habitual exercise of the authority of a master over slaves, is peculiarly destructive to the national honour and character."† When shall these just sentiments pervade the breast of every British subject in every part of the world?

Of slavery in *Dacca* the Magistrate, in 1816, observes:—"I have to state in reply, for the information of the Court of Circuit, that I have found in this court several prosecutions for inveigling away children and other persons with various intents, and they are generally females: such cases, however, in this city and district, are not very numerous. The unfortunate persons who are sold for slaves, are generally little children (females), or grown up girls that are enticed away from their parents or other relations in the Mofussil.

* Par. Papers on Slavery in India, p. 148. † p. 147.

Persons already in a state of slavery are seldom, as far as I can discover from the records of the court, or from other information, inveigled away with a view of being sold; but female slaves are often enticed away for other purposes, sometimes by men, and sometimes by women keeping houses of ill-fame. Both descriptions of offences are, I believe, *very prevalent*, especially the former, though few of them comparatively come officially to the knowledge of the Magistrate."*

Slavery in the *Carnatic* is thus described by the Moonsiffs:—"Foundlings of female slaves, of persons purchased, and of those who gratuitously yield their freedom, their posterity are slaves; absence, however long, does not alter the relative condition of master and slave; a slave, however, who is not found until after the death of his master, is not the slave of his heir. The owner of a slave is also the owner of all that slave may possess. A slave has a right to enjoy, during his life, the property which may be bequeathed to him, or of which he may in any manner become possessed, but at his death the whole becomes the property of his master. Upon the death of a slave, his master becomes the owner of all his property, whether the slave has relations or not. Owners may sell their slaves at any time."†

The registration of slaves was proposed by the Bengal Government to the Nizamut Adawlut in 1816, which intimates that the prevalence of slavery is considerable. "In preparing the draft of the proposed regulation regarding slavery, the Governor-general in Council requests that the court will take into their consideration, the expediency of requiring that *the future purchase or transfer of slaves shall be regularly registered*, and that any breach of the rules which may be framed for that purpose shall entitle the slave to demand and obtain his freedom."‡

Inquiry was made from Bombay, of the Supreme Government in Calcutta, in 1817, respecting the application of the 51st Geo. III. c. 23, relative to "the abolition of the slave trade, to domestic slaves, and the property of individuals in them; such slavery being known and legalized under the laws of both the Hindoos and Mussulmans, according to whose codes the courts are bound to administer justice." To which it was replied:—

"On this point the Vice-President in council observes, that none of the provisions of the Acts of Parliament passed for the abolition of the slave trade in any manner affect, or profess to affect, *the relation between master and slave*,

* Par. Papers on Slavery in India, p. 248. † Par Papers, 1838, p. 442. ‡ p. 249

wherever that relation may exist by law. Whatever, therefore, was the law, according to the Mahomedan and Hindoo codes (for those over whom they extend), on the subject of domestic slavery, before the passing of the Act of the 51st Geo. III. c. 23, continues to be the law still; more especially as those codes have been distinctly recognised and ordered to be observed by Parliament. At the same time it is not credible, that any intention existed to abrogate those codes, without reference to the established laws and usages of this country, and without repealing the Acts of Parliament, by which the observance of them is guaranteed to the natives. The native subjects of the British Government, residing in the territories subordinate to the several Presidencies, have, in fact, the same authority over their slaves, and the same property in them, that they would have had if the Act in question had never been passed; and the several zillah and provincial courts are bound to receive and determine all cases of that nature, which are respectively cognizable by them, under the existing regulations.

"The other points adverted to, in the documents now under consideration, relate to the conduct which should be observed on the occasion of applications being made by the subjects or governments of neighbouring states, with whom we are in amity, for the restoration of slaves who have taken refuge within the Company's territories. On this point it may be remarked, that the construction which has been uniformly given by the Supreme Government to the Act of the 51st Geo. III. c. 23, viz., that it was only intended to apply to the importation or removal of slaves by sea, would not involve any alteration in the course of proceedings hitherto adopted in similar cases. *A slave, by entering the Company's territories, does not become free; nor can he, who was lawfully a slave, emancipate himself by running away from one country where slavery is lawful, to another where it is equally lawful.* The property in the slave still continues in the master; and the master has the same right to have it restored to him that any native subjects of our territories could have, supposing that right to be established in the mode prescribed by the local laws and regulations." *

The permission of the sale of slaves in the Deccan, appears from a letter in 1819, addressed by the Political Agent in *Candeish,* to M. Elphinstone, Esq., the Commissioner. "Application having been lately made to me for permission to purchase some slaves, I took the opportunity of investigating the circumstances, which I have the honour to report for your information. It appears that the slaves were young women and girls, in the possession of some Mahratta Wunjarries, who, upon being questioned, state that they purchased them in *Berar,* from the *Tandas of the Rajpoot Brimjarrias,* who said they had got them during a late scarcity, which took place in the *Nirmut* district. Upon further investigation, I understand that the practice of carrying off children from one part of the country, to sell in another part, *is not unusual with these people.* The women appear unwilling to be sold, though they complain of their scanty food, and of the treatment they experience from their present masters. Although your letter, in answer to a former application on this subject, informed me that *no variation whatever was to be made in the existing laws regarding slaves,* yet it appears to me possible,

* Par. Papers on Slavery in India, 1828, pp. 333, 334. 1838, pp. 379—381.

that may be intended to be applied merely to the proprietary right over slaves in actual possession, and of recovering such as may desert. I request to be informed, if the practice of *carrying slaves about for sale,* of which several instances have lately been brought to my notice, is still to be permitted. In the mean time I have prohibited the sale of the young women in question till I hear from you." To which it was replied by the Commisioner:—"*The sale of slaves, as described in the above-mentioned letter, is to be permitted;* but all attempts to carry off young people by force, will be punished in the severest manner."*

"The mitigated kind of domestic slavery which prevails in the *Deccan,*" says W. Chaplin, Esq., "and has prevailed from time immemorial in most parts of India, appears to be of a description entirely different from the foreign trade in slaves, which is proscribed by recent acts of parliament, passed since the abolition of this traffic. Although it may, perhaps, be necessary to introduce some regulations to prevent the stealing or kidnapping of children, *I conceive that any restrictive measure, that should at once put a stop to the sale of slaves, would be an innovation, which would trench materially, not only on long established customs, but on the rights of private property.* Whether this species of servitude, or rather of mild bondage, is eventually to be continued under certain modifications, or to be abolished entirely, is a question which is probably now under consideration ; but as the importation of slaves from the Nizam's frontier, in consequence of the scarcity which prevails there, has of late greatly increased, the subject of your letter will be referred for the decision of the Honorable the Governor in Council. Whatever evil may result from the continuance of the traffic, it is certainly, I think, the means at the present moment of much actual good, inasmuch as it has the effect of preserving the lives of numbers of parents and children, who would otherwise perish from famine."†—Poona, Dec. 1819.

The difference of opinion and procedure of some of the Indian Magistrates, manifests the difficulty of legislation where slavery exists. This appears by some slave cases, stated by W. Leycester, Esq., Second Judge of the *Bareilly* Court of Circuit, in 1815.—

"In one case, Enayt Khaun is taken up by the police darogah, of *Bhudyke,* and sent as a prisoner to the magistrate of *Cawnpore,* for importing two female slaves, and *the magistrate discharges him, and gives him the slaves.*

* Par. Papers on Slavery in India, p. 339. † pp. 341, 342.

"In a second case, Ooda is taken up for importing a woman named Manucooer, by a police sowar, and delivered over to the police darogah of *Bindrabun*. Ooda says he bought her for *twenty-one rupees* in the Ranna's country, and she admits it, and adds, she understands he means to resell her. The acting magistrate liberates the woman.

"In a third case, Sabet Khaun is taken up by a jemmedar, and delivered over to the darogah of *Koria Gunje*. It would seem he had been sent by Assud Alee Cauzee of Jelaneh, to purchase a slave in the vicinity of Cassepore and Roderpoore (*the market for slaves imported from the hills*); but on coming to Bareilly he falls in with Besharut Khan, a slave-dealer, who, from his stock in hand, sells to him a woman named Zuhorun, twenty years of age; but the Cauzee, thinking her too old, leaves her on Sabet Khaun's hands. The assistant magistrate liberates the woman.

"In a fourth case, Nurotum is taken up by the darogah of *Nudjeebabad*. It would seem that he had purchased a woman named Anundee, for *twenty rupees*, of an inhabitant of the hills. The assistant magistrate does not liberate the woman, but takes a recognizance from Nurotum to produce her, if any other claimant should appear.

"In a fifth case, Choonee, the head of a set of dancing girls, prosecutes Hyatt Alee Cutwaul, of Amrooa, for detaining forcibly Munnuvur Jaun, one of her female slaves. Munnuvur Jaun says, she is not satisfied to remain with Choonee, and the magistrate liberates her. Choonee appeals, and produces a deed of sale for the slave, executed by Shumshere, an inhabitant of the hills. The opinion of the law officer of the Court of Circuit is taken, who declares, '*the sale of a resident of this country illegal*;' and the order of the magistrate was confirmed.

"The first case was submitted by me to the Nizamut Adawlut, with a recommendation that the said Enayt Khaun should be punished, and the slaves discharged, or sent back, as required by the 10th Regulation of 1811; and the court in reply adjudge that, under the construction given to the provisions of the 10th Regulation, 1811, *the case in question does not fall within the operation of that Regulation*; and, having referred to the court's orders, it would seem, that on a representation from Mr. Blunt, the court had decided that the regulation in question was 'applicable only to the importation of slaves for the purpose of being sold, given away, or otherwise disposed of.'"*

It appears, that when slaves have been imported, their owners have endeavoured to evade the law against the Slave Trade, by not immediately disposing of them; on which it is very justly remarked,—"Is not keeping a person imported as a slave, to be a slave, a disposal of him? What is to be said to the notorious fact of females, so imported as slaves, being let out in retail for the purposes of prostitution, and any offspring they may have being sold, *agreeably to the daily practice regarding the indigenous slaves of the country, for the benefit of the slave master?* This surely is a disposal of them and of their issue."† Is not this species of slavery equal in atrocity to the slavery of the West Indies, now so happily abolished?

"Slavery in *Malwa*," says Sir John Malcolm, "is chiefly limited to *females*; but there is, perhaps, no province in India where there are so many slaves of this sex. The dancing girls are all purchased when young by the *nakins*, or heads

* Par. Papers on Slavery in India, pp. 342, 343. † p. 344.

of the different sects, who often lay out large sums in these purchases; female children and grown up young women, are bought by all ranks. Among the Rajpoot chiefs these slaves are very numerous, as also in the houses of the principal Brahmuns; *the usage descends to the lowest ranks, and few merchants or cultivators with any property are without mistresses or servants of this description.* Male slaves are rare, and never seen but with men of some rank or property, with whom they are usually the confidential servants. There are a variety of ways in which slaves are procured in Malwa;—numbers date their condition from a famine or scarcity, when men sold their children to those who were able to support them. A great number of the slaves of Malwa are from *Rajpootana,* where the excesses of the Mahrattas drove the inhabitants to exile, and to such distress as to be compelled to part with their children. But, besides these sources of slavery, there are others of a more criminal nature. There are many instances of Rajpoots, and men of other tribes, particularly Soandees, selling the children whom they have by their slaves, and who are deemed to be born in a state of bondage. This takes place when the father is in distress, or when he is tempted by a large price. The sale of the offspring of these women by other fathers than their masters is more common. These slaves are not numerous; but the further demand is supplied by the Binjarries, who import females into and from *Guzerat and other countries,* whom they usually pretend to have bought; and by the tribe of Gwarriah, professed stealers of female children. When these slaves are bought, an inquiry is made as to their tribe, and the general answer (particularly from the Gwarriahs) is, that they are Rajpoots. The children are taught to make pretensions to high birth, and daily instances occur of whole families losing cast in consequence of their being too hastily credited. Females in Malwa, except in times of scarcity or general distress from any cause, are sold from 40 to 50, to 100 and 150 rupees; the price is accordant with their appearance. They have been, at times, an article of considerable commerce, many being annually sent to the southward, particularly to the *Poonah* territories, where they sold high. This trade, which has of late years decreased, was principally carried on by the Mahratta Brahmuns, some of whom amassed great sums by this shameless traffic."*

"It is to be feared that a large proportion of those consigned

* Par. Papers as above, Report on Malwa, 1821, pp. 414, 415.

to foreign slavery are kidnapped, that being the cheapest mode of obtaining them. It must be obvious that the employment of the slave dealer is calculated to carry either actual or apprehended distress into every village throughout the tract in which they prosecute this detestable traffic, a tract which comprises not only the whole of *Rajpootana* and *Malwa*, but extends through *Guzerat* to the sea."*

The Par. Papers contain more minute information, respecting the state of slavery under the Madras Presidency, than of the other Presidencies in India.—"In *Malabar* and *Canara*, where the land is very generally divided, and occupied as separate and distinct properties, *the labourer is the personal slave of the proprietor, and is sold and mortgaged by him, independently of his lands.* In the *Tamil* country, where land is of less value, and belongs more frequently to a community than to an individual, the labourer is understood to be *the slave rather of the soil than of its owner*, and is seldom sold or mortgaged, except along with the land to which he is attached; but in *Telingana*, where it is difficult now to trace the remains of private property in the land, this class of people is considered free. It has been stated by very competent authority, Mr. F. W. Ellis, the Collector of Madras, that in the Tamil country, the *parriyars* and *pullers*, most of whom are slaves attached to the lands of the *vallaler*, as well as the *pulli*, who are generally serfs on the lands of the Brahmun meerassidars, sometimes claim meras, or *hereditary private property*, in the 'incidents of their villainage;' and that 'it is generally allowed to them and their descendants, on proving their former residence in the village, however long they may have been absent from it.' On the other hand, the late Magistrate in Malabar, in addressing Government respecting the sale of men, women, and children of the *pollar, cherumakul, panian, kanakan, kallady, yocallan, and nacady* tribes, submits that, 'if the general question of slavery, as recognised by the local usages of Malabar, or by the Hindoo and Mahomedan law, is not affected by the laws made to abolish the Slave Trade—adverting to *the wretchedness and diminutive appearance of this description of natives*—it still appears to be a subject well worthy the humane consideration of the Right Hon. the Governor in Council, to enact such legislative provisions as will tend to ameliorate their condition, and prevent their being sold out of the talook, or, indeed, of the estate, the place of their nativity; and, above all, *from being exposed to*

* Par. Papers, 1838, p. 56.

sale by public auction, in execution of decrees, or in satisfaction of revenue demands."*

It appears to have been common, *to dispose of the slaves on an estate as a part of the real property.*—"The Hindoo law (says the Collector of *Malabar*), on the subject of transfers of property, speaks of 'land and slaves employed in the cultivation of it,' and evidently contemplates those two species of property as one and the same, and as not properly *separable from each other*. And we find that not only in this, but in other countries, it has been usual to transfer the slaves who were a '*descripti glebæ*' with the land itself. Indeed, the attachment of the Hindoos to the lands which they have always occupied, and to the village where they have always resided, is proverbial; and to separate them from their native soil, might, under such circumstances, be considered an additional act of cruelty. A certain portion of the produce of the soil which they cultivate, is, in the Tamil country, allowed by the master for the maintenance of his slaves, whose duty it is to till the ground; and, unless they were transferred with the land, the new proprietor, when he obtained possession, might experience difficulty in carrying on the cultivation, and the former master might be deprived of the means of enabling him to afford subsistence to his slaves. The probability of being transferred with the land, gives them on this coast a sort of property in their huts and little spots of ground, which they can thus occupy without any great fear of being turned out, or transferred, contrary to their interests, feeling, and comfort. It must, however, be observed, that on the other coast *universally*, and even *generally* on this coast, *slaves are not necessarily sold with the land*, although the convenience of all parts seems to have rendered the practice common."

The apathy manifested by the Collector of *Calicut* in 1819, respecting the sale of slaves for default of revenue, shows the influence of the slave system upon the most respectable of the European functionaries of Government. "In attempting to ameliorate the condition of these slaves, care must be taken that we do not increase them. The partial measure, of declaring them not liable to be sold for arrears of revenue, will be a drop of water in the ocean; though, *why Government should give up a right which every proprietor enjoys, is a question worthy of consideration.*"†

The following copious extracts from the reports of *eleven Collectors*, to whom the Madras Government had addressed

* Par. Papers on Slavery in India, p. 817. † p. 846. See p. 435.

queries respecting the state of slavery in their respective districts, appear peculiarly interesting. The whole letter, from the Secretary of Government in the revenue department, contains *fourteen folio pages,* and bears date, April, 1819.

"In SALEM slavery does not appear to exist. The Collector observes, 'I can safely state that, in the manner referred to in these communications, *there is no vestige whatever of slavery in this collectorate, nor has any such practice obtained from the time the country came into possession of the Honourable Company.* During the Mussulman government, there were a few slaves belonging to certain Nunjah lands in the vicinity of the Cauvery, and there are now some descendants of these people; but they are as free as any other inhabitants. I have heard of one or two instances of a child being sold for the purpose of domestic slavery; but this is uncommonly rare, and such a circumstance as a person being sold as a slave has never transpired.

"In MADURA and DINDIGUL slavery existed during the Mahomedan government. The slaves were sold at the pleasure of their masters, but they were not '*adscripti glebæ;*' not necessarily sold whenever the land was sold.

The Collector's words are, 'When a puller or parriah was unable to gain a livelihood, he was accustomed to offer himself or his relatives as slaves to the cultivating inhabitants, for a sum of money, varying from one to ten cully chuckrums, when a bond of slavery was drawn out and signed. If they married, *their children were considered the property of the owners.* They were employed in the cultivation of land, and were maintained by the owners, who frequently, for their services, would grant them an allowance in grain, in addition to other allowances. If the proprietor of land was obliged to dispose of the whole of his lands, he still retained possession of his slaves, and disposed of them as he pleased, as they were not considered attached to the land. If an owner was unable to maintain his slave, he could let him out to others, by which means he frequently derived a maintenance both for himself and his slave; but the slave was obliged to return to his master whenever he required him, who could mortgage or sell him at pleasure. Since the assumption of the country, some slaves continued with their masters; others have left them, and have even enlisted as sepoys. I cannot discover that any puller has sold himself as a slave of late years. *Slavery seems gradually disappearing; which may be attributed to the knowledge, that it is not encouraged in the different courts of justice.* Some pullers cultivate their own lands, and have their own puttiams. Those who cultivate the lands of others, and who are not slaves, receive a regulated hire.'

"In COIMBATORE slavery is reported to exist, 'but in a very few villages.' The Collector observes, 'From all that I can learn, it appears certain that, *the owner has a right to sell his slave without the land; but that it is a right very seldom, if ever, exercised.* The highest price for a good slave is fifty rupees; the price, however, is seldom so high. The children of slaves are born slaves. On the birth of a child, the master presents the parents with cloths, and one or two rupees. The master is supposed to be vested with despotic authority over their slaves, and with power to punish them. An apprehension, however, that the exercise of such authority is not permitted by the British government appears generally prevalent, and rather operates to prevent the merchandise of slaves, as *they are considered to be less valuable, when free from the fear of punishment.* There appears reason for thinking that the slaves are, on the whole, better treated by their masters than the common class of free labourers. The master possesses a power, *not only over the person, but over the property of his slave;* and he may make use of the cattle reared by the slave for agricultural purposes! The slaves are sold with the land; but, if they should object to serve another master, they are not forced to do so. This I take to be an indulgence of the master, not a right of the slave. The slaves have *a share of the produce allotted for their subsistence, about* AN EIGHTH. In some instances, land has been made over to the pullers, which they cultivate for their support. In many places, where slavery does not exist, a species of bondage is introduced, by the ryots undertaking *to bear the expense of their puller's marriage*, upon condition of the latter binding themselves to serve the ryots exclusively for life. Slavery may almost be considered as extinct in Coimbatore.'

"In TANJORE slavery exists; but, as in *Madura* and *Dindigul*, it is founded, in the first instance, upon voluntary contract. 'The slaves are never seized or sold for arrears of revenue. The slaves here are of two casts only, the puller and pariah; the origin of their bondage arises in a voluntary agreement, on their part, to become the slave of some other man more powerful than themselves, upon whom they thus impose a more strict obligation to protect and maintain them and their families, than if merely serving them as labouring servants. The Brahmuns, in consideration of their cast, do not receive bonds of slavery directly in their own name, but have them generally drawn out in that of some of their soodra dependents. When a bond of slavery has been given, it ceases not with the life of the party, but is *binding upon the descendants of the original giver*, who continue bound by the conditions of it. In return, the owner is obliged to find subsistence at all times, and under all circumstances, for the family of his bondsman; whom he can employ in any manner he pleases; although it is generally as a labourer in the fields. The bondsman does not reside in his master's house, nor form any part of his family, but has a house provided for him along with the others of his cast, to which a back yard of eighty goontahs rent-free is attached, the same as other labourers. *The master has the power of selling the slave, but he cannot sell him to any one who will carry him to a distant part of the country, without his own consent.* If the master, through poverty or other cause, fails or becomes unable to subsist his bondsman and his family, he is at liberty to seek employment as a free labourer, but is liable to be reclaimed at any time by his master, when he may be in a condition to fulfil his part of the agreement. When lands are sold, in any way, it is always independent of the bondsmen upon it. If they are likewise to be sold, separate deeds of transfer are passed. If not, they continue attached to their former masters. No persons of this description have ever yet been considered as seizable property, or sold for an arrear of revenue; nor do I believe ever by a judicial decree in any civil cause; nor have I ever known this species of property recognised by the officers of government, although it is by the natives themselves, in their transactions with each other.

'On the part of the bondsman, his rights are subsistence and protection for himself and family from his master, with liberty to seek it elsewhere, as a free agent, if not found him: and the right of not being removed by sale to a distant country from the place of his birth. With regard to himself, personally, his treatment from his master is the same as that of his other labourers, which is, in general, of a mild nature; but he is not more liable to personal punishment than others, in consequence of his state of bondage; and any cruelty or abuse of authority on the part of the master, towards his bondsman, would be complained against, and punished with equal strictness, as if committed upon a free man. The Board will perceive that the condition of these people differs very little from that of the common labourers. The disadvantage to the bondsman is, *the power of being sold or transferred to other masters:* and this is not very frequent, as it is the last property, generally, which is disposed of by a person in distressed circumstances. The advantages are, the more effectually securing subsistence and protection to themselves and families, particularly in times of trouble or difficulty, than it is binding on masters in general to bestow upon common labourers; and this without rendering their condition in any degree intolerable, towards the amelioration of which, the equity and mildness of the British Government have greatly operated, in respect to rendering the conduct of masters to their servants indulgent. I do not find that the system of slaves attached to the soil, and transferable by purchase as appendages to the land, obtains here.'

"TINNEVELLY. '*It is usual, in this district, for slaves to be sold or mortgaged either with the land or separately, as the proprietor pleases, or his wants require.* There is no particular rule, or general custom, by which the conduct between the master and slave, and the slave and master, is governed, except that the master has, at all times, the command of his slave's labour, and that he cannot work for any other person without the permission of his master.

'In regard to the treatment of masters towards their slaves, it does not appear to be incumbent on them to afford a subsistence except when employed in their business; and then *it is on the lowest scale of allowance*, being generally no more than two measures of paddy per day. At other times their slaves are obliged to seek a livelihood at the hands of others, being bound to return to their masters when the season of cultivation commences. Besides this allowance, which the slaves receive from their masters on working days, they are entitled, when the crops are reaped, to a small deduction from the gross produce, called here, '*Paroo*,' which varies in different villages, but *amounts generally to about* 23-8 *per cent*. It is usual, when deaths occur among them, for their masters to assist them in the necessary funeral expenses; and on marriages, births, and festival days, to grant them presents, according as their circumstances will admit; but these acts are quite voluntary on the part of the masters, and the slave can claim nothing more than a bare subsistence while he works, and his allowance, as above described, at the time of harvest.

'All punishment of the slave by the master, if this power ever existed, and was recognised in former times, seems to be at an end; and there is no instance, within my experience in this district, of a slave complaining of ill-treatment from his master. The fact, indeed, appears to be, that the slave is so necessary to the cultivation, and labourers are so scarce, that the proprietors find it their interest to treat them well; and the slaves, in time, become so attached to the village in which they are settled, that they seem not to consider their situation, nor show any desire to be free. In calling upon the tehsildars for an account of a person's property, to know whether he is a fit security for another, it is usual, if he possess slaves, to include them, a male slave being estimated in value from 3 to 15 C. Chuckrums (R 6 $\frac{93}{256}$ to 31 $\frac{29}{256}$), and a female from 3 to 5 C. Chuckrums (6 $\frac{93}{256}$ to 10 $\frac{155}{256}$), but *I have always rejected them in the account as unavailable property by the Government, and none have ever been sold in this district for an arrear of revenue*.'*

"South Arcot. The slaves in this collectorate are mostly of the Pully and Pariar casts, and the majority of them are chiefly devoted to agriculture. The number of slaves in this district, of both sexes, including children, amounts to upwards of 17,000; and they appear to have been generally born in a state of servitude, through some contract of their forefathers. The Hindoo code of laws, religious and civil, seems to declare that the Soodra tribes are naturally born in a state of servitude; and, although some of the superiors of the sub-divisions of that tribe in modern days, have emancipated themselves from this degrading thraldom, yet the lower casts are always looked upon as natural slaves, the property of any person, *who contributes to defray their marriage expenses, which is the ordinary way, at present, of constituting hereditary slavery*. Previously to the assumption of the Carnatic, the owners of slaves were empowered to punish them, either by castigation or confinement, at their discretion; but that power, subsequently to the British administration, has ceased to be exercised. The possessions and acquisitions of slaves, are generally considered the property of their

---

* "The jemn *value of a good Parier*, as well as a good Addian (slave), is thirty rupees; Otty, twenty-seven and a half rupees; Kanom, fifteen rupees; and the jemn value of a less able one of either tribe, is twenty rupees; Otty, seventeen and a half rupees; Kanom, ten rupees; and Paneyam, eight rupees. The jemn value of children (male) of those sects is twelve rupees. The jemn value of a female slave, of any of the two tribes above mentioned, as well as of their female children, is three rupees and eighty reas. The jemn value of a good Poolean slave is twelve rupees; Otty, ten rupees; and Kanom, six rupees; and the jemn value of a less able one, eight rupees; Otty, six rupees; Kanom, four rupees. The value of a good Panian or Addian (slave), might be said to have increased, by five rupees, above the old price, but that of the Naiken, Moorpan, and Poliar, continues still the same." (Par. Papers, 1828, pp. 852, 853.)

masters, who, however, usually relinquish them to the family of the slave. Slaves cannot enter into any matrimonial connexion without the consent of their owners, who, as they defray the expenses of the marriage, virtually revive the contract of hereditary bondage; for *the offspring of slaves are always regarded as the property of their father's owner.*

'It is stated that the slaves of this district can be sold by their owners to any person, and to an alien village, and that no slaves are attached to any particular soil or village. But I am induced to believe that such a practice is at variance with the rights annexed to the state of real bondage; for in some Meerassi villages it is known that the Meerassidars have advanced pretensions to possess an equal proportion of the slaves with their share of the villages, and I also believe that such a practice is hardly ever resorted to. The price of a male slave and family, when sold by their owner to another person, varies considerably, and ranges from *ten to fifty pagodas.* The owners of slaves are required to provide them with food and clothing, to defray their wedding expenses, and to assist them on the births of children, and in their funeral charges. The food differs according to the opulence of the owner, but is always sufficient for subsistence, or the owner permits the slave to serve elsewhere during his poverty. The clothing is very scanty, except when the slaves are chiefly employed for domestic purposes; and I cannot discover that the apparel is designedly calculated to portray the class of the wearers. The duties of slaves are to attend the cattle and agriculture, and to assist in domestic services, connected with the house or person of their owners.

'It does not appear that *enfranchisement of slaves ever takes place.* Yet as some owners have been reduced to indigence, and are unable to employ or subsist their hereditary slaves, those persons are ostensibly free, and labour for any person who will employ them. Cases of emancipation occur in the extinction of the owners' families; and from this description of Soodras, who still sacrifice their liberties, modern slaves are constituted; for they are mostly very needy, and consent to perpetual and hereditary bondage for about twenty or thirty pagodas, which the cultivator advances for the celebration of the marriage ceremony. In no instance, I believe, do engagements exist, where a *labourer discharges such a loan by his manual labour.*'

"Chingleput. 'The slaves employed in the cultivation of the lands, and to which this report principally refers, have, for the most part, their allowances regularly rendered; so much grain being granted to each labourer, and a proportionate subsistence to each of his children or others of the family. They are housed and clothed; and, during the principal festivals, certain allowances are made them both in money and articles required for their ceremonies. Their marriages are also performed at the charge of their masters; and, when reduced by infirmity, they are also supported by their proprietors. The condition of this description of people, composing the chief part of the Pariahs of the district, has, of late years, considerably changed. This may, in a great measure, arise from the vicinity of their situation to Madras, *where this system is known to be abrogated.* Many of them there obtain employment, and their proprietors would find it difficult to reclaim them. The regulations have so far circumscribed the authority formerly exercised by the proprietors, that they cannot keep them under control. The proprietors finding themselves very incapable of employing their services, or rather controlling them as arbitrarily as before, complain less of the loss of this description of property. The slaves are also possessed by many of the Vellairs, &c., who have long since established themselves in the cultivation of particular villages; but their situation, in such cases, is similar to those in the service of other soodras. *The sale of slaves has been, I believe, of late years, discontinued, or of very rare occurrence*; and in these parts no attachment of such property has ever been made on account of the dues of government.'

"Trichinopoly.—'In the wet districts of Trichinopoly, the number of pullers may be stated at 10,000, including those employed for the purpose of watching and feeding the cattle. In the dry districts, there are about 600; *but pullers are only to be found in those villages where there is paddy cultivation.* The pullers of the dry districts appear to be liable to the same rules, and to possess the same rights, as those of the wet districts. The services they perform are chiefly confined to the irrigation of the land in its several stages of cultivation; but their services are also occasionally required by their masters, in the menial offices of their household establishment. If a wall is required, *the pullers are obliged to erect it, without any further recompense than their established emoluments.* The pullers are usually sold with the land; but there are many cases in which they may be purchased independent of it. The price of a puller varies from *five to ten pagodas,* according to his age and qualifications. Their services are also occasionally mortgaged; a pullee, or female slave, is never sold; while it would appear that, *in Malabar, men, women, and children, are sold indiscriminately.*'

'The pullers are supposed to be entirely supported by their masters, in sickness and in health. Their marriages are made at the expense of the meerassidars, as well as the expense of their funerals. They enjoy some little gratuity at every birth, and receive a certain established sum at the principal Hindoo festivals. I have noted *a list of the yearly emoluments a puller is properly entitled to receive;* and these emoluments, though small, I have every reason to believe, are scarcely ever withheld.*

'I have examined the pullers themselves, on the subject of their being well or ill treated, and asked them what course they would pursue if ill used. They replied, *they would seek other masters at a distance, that would treat them more kindly.* In corroboration of this fact I have never received a complaint, either in my fiscal or magisterial capacity, since my appointment to this district, from a puller against his master. The right of the puller is so distinctly defined by custom, and the interest of the meerassidar so substantially affected by the good conduct and health of the puller,—that it is hardly possible to suppose the meerassidars would be so blind to their own interest as to cause their pullers to abscond, or by harsh treatment reduce them to sickness. From what has been already stated, it will be found, that *agricultural slavery has existed in this district from time immemorial.*'

"CANARA.—'The origin of slavery in Canara is to be traced from extracts in an ancient book, called Sheehadry Pooranum, but by no means an authentic re-

---

* "The extent of cultivation to be made by a puller and by a pullee, is 150 cullums of paddy.

Annual Emoluments.	ru.	an.	
Warum of a puller culs	8	$5\frac{3}{8}$	
Do. of a pullee	6	$6\frac{3}{4}$	
Batta at the commencement of each fusly for ploughing	2	4	
Soluntrums for sowing	0	6	
Reaping share a' 5 per cent.	7	6	
Thrashing do.	1	0	
Pongal feast	1	0	
Duparaly do.	0	$0\frac{1}{8}$	
Gramadava do.	0	$1\frac{1}{2}$	
Total annual	26	$1\frac{1}{8}$	$5\frac{5}{8}$ fs.
Proposed addition of warum a' 2 per cent.	3	0	0
	29	$1\frac{1}{8}$	$5\frac{5}{8}$ fs.
Contingencies estimated:			
For a marriage	4	0 rs.	8
For a birth	0	2 fs.	2
For a death	0	2 fs.	2
	4	4 rs.	8 4
Total	33	$5\frac{5}{8}$ rs.	9 fs. $1\frac{1}{8}$"

cord. This treatise is stated to contain a fabulous narrative, which, when divested of its oriental imagery and metaphors, will be found to attribute the origin of slavery in Canara to the right of conquest.

'*The right of sale was, and is still, the master's exclusive privilege, either with or without the land.* The price varies, and is settled amongst the purchasers and sellers. The usual rates are as follow :—

'For a strong young man, from *twelve to twenty-six rupees.*

'For a strong young woman, *twelve to twenty-four rupees.*

'For a child, never under *four rupees.*

'It is customary to pass a bill of sale, on a bargain being made, or a mortgage bond. The transfer, by purchase or gift (in charity, or to the temple), is attended with a short ceremony, between the seller or giver, and receiver, and the slave. The slave drinks some water from his brass basin, and calls out, '*I am now your slave for ever.*' The zillah court has guaranteed this right by decrees, both on transfer of landed property and on sale in execution of decrees. The master can lend his slaves out on hire. *He can sell the husband to one person, and the wife to another!* This is not often done, because neither of the purchasers can be sure of keeping his purchase. Care is always taken in purchasing not to carry the slave to any distant estate. *The master can sell the children*; but this is seldom done from the foregoing cause, the fear of desertion. The master, according to his means, feeds and clothes his slaves. He *never pays them wages in money*, but presents them, on their marriages or particular ceremonies, with a small sum. The quantity of food and clothing to a slave varies in every talook. It does not seem to be *regulated by any rule*, although it would appear that some original quantum obtained. The average may be thus estimated :—

	FOOD.	CLOTHING.
A man	½ Canara seer coarse rice, two rupees weight salt, a little beetel nut and leaf.	Two pieces of cauthey, six cubits. In some talooks, a coombly and roomal given.
A woman	1 seer.	1 do. seven cubits long.
A child	¾ do.	1 do. four do.

'The salt, beetel, &c., is *optional.* It is also customary to give them conjee from the master's house. I cannot learn that any want or cruelty is experienced by the slaves, the master being well aware that, on any ill-treatment, they will desert him; and that the trouble and expense attending their recovery would, perhaps, amount to the value of the deserters. *Slavery seems to be inconsistent with rights and privileges.* On these points I can only generally state, that *the dhers of Canara possess none.* The number of slaves of all descriptions in Canara, has never been correctly ascertained; they may be estimated at 82,000.'

"MALABAR.—In Malabar (exclusive of Wynaud*) the number of slaves is estimated by the Collector at 100,000. 'They are,' says the Collector, '*slaves of the soil*, and are generally attached to the land of the proprietors of the ground on which they were born; but this is by no means considered an essen-

* "The landed proprietors of Wynaud are torpid to a degree; all the field work is done by slaves called Paniers, who are held in higher estimation than the slaves of the lower districts. They are admitted *to the threshold of their masters' houses, and they are even employed in grinding rice for the use of the temples.*" (Par. Papers, p. 924.) Hamilton thus describes *the ceremonies of respect in Malabar* :—" A nair (soldier), may approach, but not touch a Brahmun. A tair (cultivator), remains 36 yards off. A puliar (slave), 96 steps off. A tair is to remain 12 steps from a nair; a meliar 3 or 4 steps farther, a poliar 96 steps. A meliar may approach, but not touch a tair. A polier is not to come near a malear or other cast. If he wish to speak to a Brahmun or other, he must stand at the above prescribed distances and cry aloud. Formerly a nair was expected instantly to cut down a tair or musna (fisherman), who defiled him by touching him; and the same fate awaited the poliar or pariar who did not turn out of the road for the nair!!" (Ham. Hind., vol. ii., pp. 278, 280.)

tial point, being frequently transferred by sale, mortgage, or hire. *In Malabar, as in the West Indies, a man's wealth is as much appreciated by the number of his slaves, as by any other property he may possess!* In one sect they observe what is termed makkatye; in another they observe the marra makkatye; the former, being the common laws of kindred, the latter similar to the customs among the nairs, in which inheritance goes to the *sister's son*, and this constitutes the value of a female of one cast over that of the male; and, *vice versa*, a male being more valuable *where the progeny goes with him.* The marriage contract is made entirely among the parents of the parties, without any interference on the part of the proprietor; to whom, however, it is necessary to make the proposed connexion.

'No valuable consideration is given to the owner by the male for the possession of the female. *The contract may be dissolved at the pleasure of the parties connected*; in which event the husband takes off the marriage necklace (commonly composed of shells or brass ornaments), which makes the dissolution complete, and each is at liberty to form new connexions. But whilst the contract lasts I have had opportunities in my magisterial capacity, when an assistant in the courts, of observing a wonderful degree of jealousy and tenaciousness of family honour, when contrasted with the general appearance, habits, and apparently brutish stupidity of these casts. *The measure of subsistence to be given by the proprietor is fixed*, and he is bound by the prescribed customs of the country to see it served daily. A frequent failure on the part of the master to perform this duty, is sure to be attended with desertion to another, from whom they expect kinder usage; and, when this takes place, the recovery of them is attended with difficulties that are not easily overcome; for, independent of being obliged to have recourse to courts of justice, *months and years perhaps elapse before they can discover to what place the slave has absconded.* The proprietor feels it his interest to see them well treated, through apprehensions of the consequence of an opposite conduct.

'I do not recollect any instance of a churma having appealed to a court of justice for protection from the ill usage of his master; but instances are not wanting of persons having been brought to justice and to a severe account for the murder or wounding of a slave; and as it is universally known throughout Malabar that British justice considers the life of the lowest individual as valuable as the highest character in the country, and that as severe a retribution would fall on the head of the murderer of a slave as of a rajah, we may consider them as well protected by the laws as any other race of beings. In some respects, churmas may be considered in more comfortable circumstances than any of the lower and poorer class of natives. An instance of a churma being a beggar is unheard of: they and their families are sure of having the means of subsistence, for if the owner should be unable to afford this, he will sell, mortgage, or hire his churma to another, on whom would devolve the duty, as well as interest, of affording him such subsistence as to enable him to go through the labours of the day.'" *

---

* Par. Papers on Slavery in India, 1828, pp. 887—900. See also Par. Papers, 1838, pp. 383—386.

"The churmas in Malabar are *absolute property; they are part of the live stock on an estate.* In selling and buying land it is not necessary that they should follow the soil; both kinds of property are equally disposable, and may fall into different hands. The churmas may be sold, leased, and mortgaged, like the land itself, or like any cattle or thing. The feumokar may hire them for pattom or rent independently of the land, or he may sell them altogether with his estate. The jenmokar, by the ancient laws of Malabar, is *accountable to no person for the life of his own churma.* He is the legal judge of his offences, and may punish them by death, if they should appear to deserve it. The kolloonaven can neither put to death a churma, nor sell him, but he may chastise him. In the same manner as the soil, the possession of churmas, was originally confined to a particular class. They were then employed entirely in the labours of agriculture; but, although they were the first and sole cultivators in Malabar, it is not to be

To the above may be added the Report of the Collector of the NORTHERN DIVISION OF ARCOT.—

"The slaves in the district are not numerous; exhibiting a total of 688, inclusive of men, women, and children. The practice of keeping them may be said to be confined to the five talooks of *Arcot, Trevultoor, Cauvareeput, Poloor, and Suttawaid;* for in *Sholungar* and *Wondawash* (the two other talooks in which, according to the statement, slavery prevails) their numbers are very small indeed They are ostensibly employed in agriculture, and the pasturing of cattle, although they may occasionally do house work; and the persons in whose service they are principally engaged, are the Rajah, Brahmun, and Vellemwar casts. Children, born when their parents are in a state of slavery, become slaves also. It does not appear to be *accurately settled to whom the child of a slave belongs.* In one talook, it was said to the master of the male, in another to the master of the female slave; the question, perhaps, has never been agitated; for the people who keep slaves, most likely *find it cheaper to buy than to rear them!* and the offspring, when left to their parents' charge, *who have barely sufficient to support themselves, die of absolute want!* They have not any particular marks whereby they may be distinguished, except it is their wretched appearance; they are fed and clothed and subsisted entirely by their masters; their food consists of *raggy,* the coarsest kind of grain, and their clothing is a common cumly. I cannot discover that *they have any rights or privileges, and they are not possessed of any property, neither can they inherit any.*" *

The latter part of the Par. Papers, 1828, refers to *the practice of stealing children,* which appears "very prevalent at Madras." "I beg," says the Magistrate at *Tinnevelly,* "to bring officially to notice a custom which is, I believe, more or less prevalent throughout the *Madras* territories, and, as far as my observation has gone, is very frequent in the district of *Tinnevelly.* The practice I allude to, is the sale and purchase of female children by dancing women, for the avowed purpose of bringing them up to a life of immorality. The custom is so notorious, and its tendency so evident, that no comment can be necessary; but I am apprehensive that, unless it be specially excepted from those purchases of children which are now (under some circumstances) legal, an opinion may be entertained that such dealings are countenanced by law. A prohibition of such transactions could not be complained of as an infringement of any acknowledged rights; it would serve as a check upon child-stealing, which is occasionally practised under the pretence of purchase, and the public expression of the will of the Government could not but have a beneficial tendency to promote morality."†

The reply to this communication, by the Secretary of Government at Madras, it is presumed, cannot be read without

---

imagined that this is the case at present, since there are many kuddians of all casts, who cultivate their own lands."—(Walker's Report on Malabar. Par. Papers, p. 866.)

* Par. Papers on Slavery in India, pp. 873, 874. † pp. 934, 935.

feelings of strong disapprobation. "It is understood from your letter, that in the opinion of the judges of the Foujdaree Adawlut, no new enactment is required upon this subject, because the selling or purchasing of children, for the avowed purpose of prostitution, may be punished under the law as it at present stands. The Governor in Council entirely concurs with the judges in deeming any enactment unnecessary; and is further of opinion, adverting to the nature of the institution of dancing women, and to its connection with the ceremonies and observances, both religious and civil, of the great bulk of the people, and if it is at all expedient for the offices of Government to interfere, for the purpose of preventing parents or guardians from assigning children in the customary modes to be brought up to this profession, the interference requires to be conducted with the greatest caution. The remarks, to which reference is made, relate to the practice of selling children to be made slaves, and generally to the usages of the country with respect to slavery; and, it was observed, that that subject was one of much difficulty and delicacy. The subject now under consideration is of no less delicacy, and it seems to afford less inducement to interfere; for it is to be considered, that loss of personal freedom is not among the consequences of being brought up to be a dancing woman, and that the species of immorality which the interference would propose to redress prevails—is generally tolerated—in the most enlightened and most highly civilized nations of Europe, and is much more closely connected with general depravity and with misery in England than it is in India."*

It has been very forcibly observed by two of the judges of *Trichinopoly*, in 1832:—"That the slavery of the dancing girls is only in name, may be applied to the other classes, but the turpitude is in the abduction of children from their country, family, and home, for the purpose of devoting them to sensual as well as idolatrous purposes; the whole, from its origin to its consummation, is iniquitous. No subsequent kind treatment and protection can redeem or atone for the first act of abduction and all that follows it; being reconciled to a vicious course of life in no way justifies the traffic or the practice."† How lamentable that such a state of society should exist, especially that it should be palliated by a professedly Christian government!

The *present state of the melioration of slavery*—for the

* Par. Papers on Slavery in India, pp. 935. See also pp. 901—903.

† Par. Papers, 1838, p. 388.

general abolition of it is not attempted—appears in an extract of a letter from the Hon. Court of Directors to the Governor of Madras, in 1824.—"In the districts subject to your Presidency, the rights and obligations of master and slave appear to be very indistinctly defined: and this obscurity of the law we apprehend to be favourable to the slaves; for, whatever the legal power of masters may be, their actual control over the liberties of those persons who are nominally their slaves appears to be but small. *We desire that you will be extremely cautious, in making any regulation for defining the relations of master and slave. It is our wish to improve the condition of the latter to the utmost extent, and we fear that, in defining the power of masters, acts of compulsion might be legalized, which by custom are not now tolerated, and the slaves might be placed in a worse condition than before.* We shall defer making any further remarks on the subject, till we receive a further communication from you."*

To this, *nearly two years* after, the Governor in Council refers with approbation. "The opinions and views stated in these paragraphs coincide with those entertained by us."† (Feb., 1826.) Thus the state of slavery in India, which at one time is represented as mild and scarcely needing attention, at another is considered of such a nature, that the Government is afraid to touch the subject—even to "define the relations of master and slave." Is this the way to eradicate one of the greatest evils incident to mortal man? "Surely," said the late Bishop Heber, "we are, in matters of religion, the most lukewarm and cowardly people on the face of the earth."‡ Is it not equally true, as it respects the interests of humanity in India? How dreary is the prospect of the abolition of slavery in India.

Colonel James Welsh very freely expressed his opinion on the subject.—"From *Cape Comorin* to *Goa*, including Wynaad and Loonda, I believe that there were nearly 300,000, and, from the nature of the cast distinctions, by far the greater numbers were field slaves. The general condition of the agrestic slaves is bad everywhere. They enjoy little comfort, have coarse, precarious, and scanty food, frequently none at all, and no provision, that ever I could learn, for old age or sickness. The domestic slaves are, for the most part, better off, but still subject to the despotic will of their owners in every thing short of life. Their morals, like their persons,

* Par. Papers on Slavery in India, p. 901. † p. 901.
‡ Jour., vol. ii. p. 465.

are wretchedly debased. They may be seized and sold for debts in native states, but not in an English settlement. Amelioration ought certainly to be put in practice, and time will then render emancipation a blessing to all. The measures which occur to me as proper and to be immediately adopted, are, the promulgation of laws to afford protection to the slaves, apportioning their food and clothing, giving them the Sabbath day in every English settlement; *declaring children of slaves to be free born;* and utterly prohibiting the traffic in future."* —Nov., 1832.

The extent of slavery in India, at the present period, it is presumed, cannot be ascertained by the Parliamentary Documents now before the public. No census or general registration of the slaves appears to have been taken; it is only, therefore, from occasional remarks by the Magistrates, or the more regular statements of some of the Collectors under the Madras Presidency, that any probable estimate can be taken of the extent of slavery in the British dominions in the East. By the publication of these volumes of Parliamentary Papers on Slavery in India, sufficient information is given to urge the full development of the nature and extent of this system, and to excite the friends of humanity to increased exertion, till Britain, in all her dominions, regards the divine injunction, "*Let the oppressed go free, and break every yoke.*"

The second Judge of *Dacca,* in 1812, remarks, respecting that district,—"Inveigling away and selling slaves, has long been a prevailing offence, I believe, peculiar to this district, and numerous prosecutions are consequently preferred for recovering them."† The same gentleman observes, respecting *Sylhet,*—"The odious practice of trafficking in slaves has long subsisted in that zillah, and doubtless many abuses have been committed under the cloak of an authorized commerce, or, at least, of such mercantile transactions not specially prohibited. The trade is carried on to a considerable extent, as is universally acknowledged; and, from the best information on the subject, it is computed, that *the number of slaves in the district amounts to about* ONE-SIXTH *of the whole population;* and this number *progressively increases,* as their offspring are also born slaves. It is impossible to form a correct calculation of the number of slaves annually exported from the district, but it is believed to be much less considerable than formerly.‡

Of *Sylhet* and *Backergunge,* the Magistrate, J. W. Sage, Esq., in 1816, observes,—"During the ten months I was at

* Par. Papers, 1832, pp. 570—572. † Par. Papers, 1828, p. 242. ‡ p. 244.

Sylhet, I often heard that some persons gained a livelihood by enticing boys and girls (whose parents were free) from their houses in the district, and from the adjoining territories of Kackar and Jynteah, disposing of some to wealthy natives in the district, and carrying others for sale to other places. It is a common practice amongst the lower class of native women, on the loss of their husbands, or at the time of a scarcity of grain, both in Sylhet and this district (Backergunge) *to sell their children;* by which the mothers gain a livelihood, and the children are better taken care of by their new masters. Some mothers sell their female children to prostitutes; sales of that description are always made known to the police darogahs, whose duty it is to convey the parties instantly to the Magistrate, that they may be punished for so nefarious a transaction. There are some whose families have been in a state of slavery for the last hundred years, and who, *when a sale of an estate takes place, are included in the purchase;* as, however, many suits are instituted in the Sylhet district for slaves, and appeals are admitted by the court of appeal, I do not suppose Sir R. K. Dick had it in contemplation to draw the attention of government to that class of people. It might, in some measure, prevent illicit transactions, if every one, purchasing a child, was, under pain of a heavy fine and imprisonment, ordered to register such sale, and enter into an agreement at the court at the time of registering, binding himself to produce at the court the boy or girl he may buy, whenever the Magistrate should call upon him."*

"There are (says the philanthropic Judge of Bundlecund, J. Richardson, Esq.) districts under the Company's dominions, particularly *Ramghur,* where, to my own knowledge, the greatest part of the labourers are slaves. I have no scruple to avow, I deem this one great cause of the uncultivated condition of the country, and the barbarous state of its inhabitants; for what human being will labour with good will, or a desire of improvement, when another enjoys the sole produce?"† This gentleman further observes,—"By an enforcement of the spirit and principles of the Mussulman law, a total stop would be put to the practice of slavery, which, almost incredible to state, *exists contrary to law and reason, throughout our dominions in India, to a degree scarcely to be believed;* not a Mussulman family, of even mediocrity, that has not numbers both of male and female slaves. The people about their persons, and the female attendants on their women, are almost

* Par. Papers on Slavery in India, 1828, p. 247. † p. 300.

all slaves; and, to my certain knowledge, they have slaves for the purpose of cultivation and field labour."*

Hamilton, in his *Description of Hindostan,* thus speaks of slavery.—" Domestic slavery is very generally prevalent in *Bengal,* among both Hindoos and Mahomedans. More trusty than hired servants, slaves are almost exclusively employed in the house, for attendance on the members of the family, and in all the most confidential services. Every opulent person, every one raised above the condition of the simplest mediocrity, is provided with household slaves, and from this class chiefly are taken the concubines of Mahomedans and Hindoos. In the lower provinces, under the Bengal presidency, the *employment of slaves in the labours of husbandry is almost unknown.* In the upper provinces, beginning from *Western Behar* and *Benares,* the petty landlords, who are themselves cultivators, are aided in their husbandry by slaves, whom they very commonly employ as herds and ploughmen; landlords of a higher class have in a few instances the pretensions of masters over a part of their tenants long settled on their estates, and reputed to be descended from persons who were the acknowledged slaves of their ancestors. Their claims to the services of these hereditary serfs, who are scarcely to be distinguished from the rest of the peasantry, are nearly obsolete and scarcely attended with any practical consequences; but those employed in husbandry by the inferior classes of landlords are decidedly slaves. The employment of slaves in handicraft work is more rare, but not entirely unknown. It would be difficult to form a computation of the number of slaves throughout the country, and any steps towards the preparation of an accurate estimate would involve inquiries which cannot fail of exciting great alarm. Slaves are neither so few as to be of no consideration, nor so numerous as to constitute a notable proportion of the population. The slave is more usually a favourite and confidential servant than an abject drudge; and he is held superior to the hireling both in his master's estimation and his own."†

"A portion of the population of the district of *Tiperah* are slaves, and the custom of disposing of persons already in a state of slavery is common throughout the district. On these occasions regular deeds of sale are executed, some of which are registered in the court of justice; and when an estate, to which slaves are attached, is sold privately, the slaves are

* Par. Papers on Slavery in India, p. 317.

† Hamilton's Hind., vol. i. pp. 105—107.

commonly sold at the same time, although a separate deed of sale is always executed."*

"Among the domestics in *Rungpore* are both male and female slaves, especially towards *Assam*, and everywhere along the northern frontier. The people of Assam sell many slaves, and those of *Cooch Bahar* are not unwilling to carry on the same trade."†

"Slaves in *Dinagepore* are very few, and were mostly purchased during the great famine in 1769, and the scarcity of 1787, to keep them from starving; but they turned out so idle and careless, that their labour was found much more expensive than that of hired labourers."‡

"In the district of *Purnea* are various classes of slaves; of which one class costs from £1 15s. to £2 5s.; in another class a youth costs from £1 8s. to £2 5s., and a girl of eight years, from 11s. to £1 15s. They are allowed to marry, and their children become slaves, but the family are seldom sold separately."§

"Real slaves of the male sex in *Boglipore*, are called nufur, and their women laundies. They may be sold in whatever manner the master chooses, but they are not often brought to market. The slaves here are in general industrious, seldom run away, and are rarely beaten."‖

In *Behar* "slaves of the description of nufur and laundi, are very numerous, often liberated, seldom sold, and frequently, owing to the poverty of their owners, left to find a subsistence for themselves. In *Gya*, and some other places, slaves are occasionally sold, and formerly fetched a *rupee* for each year of their age, until they reached twenty, when they attained their highest value. *In general the price has recently greatly risen.*"¶

"Theft is common throughout *Ramghur*, but murder more prevalent among a particular class, which are *the slaves* possessed by persons inhabiting the mountainous and inaccessible interior, and of savage and ferocious habits. When petty disputes occur, *these slaves are compelled by their masters to perpetrate any enormity, and are more especially employed for the purposes of assassination!* Any hesitation or repugnance on the part of the slave, is attended with immediate death, which is equally his fate should he fail in the attempt. If he succeed, he is sought out by the officers of Government, and

* Hamilton's Hind., 1821, vol. i. p. 182. Of *Sylhet*, see p. 196.
† p. 207. ‡ p. 223. § p. 234. ‖ p. 248. ¶ p. 258.

executed as a murderer. The usual police have hitherto been unable to seize the cowardly instigator, and if recourse be had to a military force, he retires into the jungles. On the occurrence of such an event, the whole country is thrown into confusion and rebellion, during which many unoffending persons lose their lives; and the troops, after many ineffectual efforts to execute the Magistrate's orders, return to their stations, worn out with fatigue, and their numbers thinned by the pestilential atmosphere of the jungles. Neither do the slaves attach the slightest idea of guilt to the murders they are thus delegated to commit; on the contrary, when seized, they always confess, and appear to expect applause for having done their duty."*

"Slaves are common in *Afghanistan*, mostly home-born, the rest imported. *Abyssinians* and *Negroes* are sometimes brought from Arabia through the ports of *Sinde;* the *Baloochees* sell Persians, and other prisoners; and many Caffres are purchased or made prisoners. The Caffre captives are generally females, and much sought after on account of their beauty."†

"Slaves are much employed in agriculture at *Malari* in *Kumaon*, and used to be purchased here by the Gorkhas."‡

"In *Nepaul*," says Hamilton, "most of the domestic servants are slaves; and there are some Brahmuns who are slaves to Rajpoots, and, in high familes, are employed as cooks (an office of great dignity), or in the service of public chapels. All other ranks are sold for common slaves, and persons of the best family have been degraded by the Raja, and given to *damais* or tailors; by which they not only lose their liberty, but also their cast, which, to a Hindoo, is of much more importance, as in general among the higher classes, the cast of a slave is respected. It is reckoned very disgraceful to sell their children to any person of impure birth, or to an infidel, yet in cases of exigence it is frequently done, and the parents do not lose cast, which, however, they inevitably would, if they afterwards received their child into their house, even were he liberated by his master. All the female slaves, or *Keties*, not excepting those belonging to the Queen, are prostitutes, although the latter are allowed some privileges, and have considerable influence at court. In the day time they attend the Queen, and when she goes out, some of them,

* p. 284. See an account of *Goomsur*, in the Northern Circars, vol. ii. p. 70.

† p. 543.

‡ p. 661.

armed with swords, follow her on horseback, and form her body guard; on which occasions they are dressed and ride on horseback like men."*

Respecting *Assam*, contiguous to Bengal, it is also stated,—"Capital punishments extend to the whole family of a rebel—parents, sisters, wife, and children; and it is probable, from these sources that the rafts are supplied, which are frequently seen floating down the Brahmaputra, past *Goalpara*, covered with human heads. All the domestics are slaves and they are numerous; every man of rank having several, mostly procured among the necessitous, who mortgage themselves. Some are exported, and about 100, of pure cast, are annually sold in Bengal. The girls chiefly are bought by professional prostitutes, and cost from twelve to fifteen rupees. A Cooch boy costs twenty-five rupees; a Kolita, fifty; slaves of impure tribes are also to the Garrows."†

"The tract, at present occupied by the *Independent Garrows*, cannot be estimated at more than 130 miles in length, by 30 in broadth. Rungta, one of the principal Garrow Chiefs, died many years ago, and was succeeded by his son Agund, who is still alive, and is said to possess great wealth *in slaves, brass pots, and human skulls!* This chief attended the marriage of the Zemindar of Currybarry's son, when a palanquin was presented to him; which, having first deprived of the poles as useless, he entered, and was borne away over the hills, on the heads of his slaves. On the death of a highland chief, of common rank, the head of one of his slaves should be burned with him; but if he be a chief of great dignity, a large body of his slaves sally out from the hills, and seize a Hindoo, whose head they cut off, and burn along with the body of their chieftain."‡

"Slavery seems to have been sanctioned by immemorial usage in the hill districts of *Kumarn* and *Gurhwal*. The uncivilized condition of the people under the Hindoo government caused no degradation to be attached to a state of bondage, and human beings were bought or sold like cattle, whenever avarice prompted, or necessity compelled a recourse to the practice. These slaves continued for generations in the same family, or were transferred by sale or other mode of conveyance, from one owner to another, in a state of permanent bondage."—(Feb., 1836.)§ Some melioration of slavery in this part of India is in progress.

* Hamilton's Hind., vol. ii p. 680. † p. 744. ‡ p. 762.
§ Par. Papers, 1838, p. 360.

The state of the slave trade in *Pulo Nias*, in 1821, is decribed in "*The Life of Sir S. Raffles.*"—"The number of slaves taken from Nias, in each year, exceed 1,500. The circumstances attending this inhuman traffic, were of the most appalling nature. Sir Stamford Raffles, then Governor of Bencoolen, in the immediate neighbourhood, was anxious to do the utmost possible good for such a people. He warmly advocated the receiving this island under the protection of the British flag, and the immediate suppression of the slave trade, and hoped so great a benefit, so easily obtained, would be met with approbation by all the wise and good. But the Court of Directors of the East India Company, 'had no hesitation in declaring that his proceedings, with regard to Pulo Nias, were deserving of their decided reprehension;' and, 'they were inclined to visit him with some severe mark of their displeasure for the steps he had taken,' and threatened to remove him from his government. After the transfer of Sumatra to the Dutch, the slave trade was resumed with greater vigour than ever, and numbers of these poor people have since been carried away to *Batavia* and *Bourbon*."*

It appears that Suttee exists in the *Island of Bali*,† or little Java, and it is painful to state, that slavery also is found, and even encouraged by European governments.

"Slavery may be said to exist in *Bali*, as all malefactors among the men, and all unfortunates among the women, become immediately the slaves of the king. Some of these he employs in working for him, and some he sends out to trade, on condition of their bringing him a certain portion of the profits. Some, when old and useless, or flagrant offenders, *are creesed out of the way*: and some of better promise are sold to the Chinese, who dispose of them to the Dutch, or to French vessels, visiting the different sea-ports. Prisoners taken in war may be dealt with in the same way; and poor unprotected persons, who have no relatives to befriend them, are in danger of sharing the same fate. At *Bali Badong*, a person was established, on behalf of the *Netherlands* Government, to buy up these people and transport them to Java, to be employed as soldiers in the Dutch service. The contract was, it appears, for 1,000 fighting men, at twenty dollars a head; about one half of this number has been supplied during the last two years, who have cost the government, including agency and transport, about 20,000 dollars. No persons are chosen for this purpose but young able-bodied men, the old,

* World Paper, Oct. 3, 1831.

† See India's Cries, 3rd edit., p. 270.

infirm, and deformed, being rejected; and as soon as a sufficient number are collected together, the colonial cruizers come to take them away. Last year, two French ships came from the Mauritius, one to Badong, and the other to Penang Cove, to buy slaves. These preferred women, and valued them according to their youthful and plump appearance; for young women they gave generally 150 rupees, 80 for the middle aged, and rejected the old ones. Boys were also bought by them, but they seldom took grown-up men, as they might prove too stiff and stubborn for their management. These vessels took away about 500 slaves between them, and talked of coming again; the time of their arrival is generally in the beginning of the year, and of their return in March. With respect to the traffic of these French vessels, there can be no demur in denouncing it as a regular slave trade, deserving to be reprobated and punished. The Netherlands Government and their agent may, perhaps, designate the transactions in which they are engaged by some other name; they may, perhaps, call it redeeming these poor people out of slavery, or rescuing them from a still worse doom; but to the impartial observer it would appear very nearly allied to it."*

The Resident in the *Persian Gulf*, in March, 1831, gave an affecting account of slavery and the slave-trade, at *Muscat, Rasal, Khyma, the Island of Bharein, Bushire, in Persia*, &c. "From 1,400 to 1,700 male and female slaves are in general annually imported into Muscat. About three-fourths are imported by sea from Sawahel, on the coast of Africa, the remaining are Abyssinians, brought by sea from Zemen, in Arabia. The mortality on board the vessels which convey these slaves is sometimes very considerable; when the small-pox breaks out it is always very great." "I repeat my conviction," says H. Pottinger, Esq., "that it is only by getting his Highness the Imam of Muscat to prevent the exportation of slaves, that we shall ever succeed in checking it."†—Oct. 1836.

Slavery exists in "its most hideous shape" in the Island of *New Zealand;* and the author of a recent work, relative to this island, very justly remarks—"That slavery should be the custom of savage nations and cannibals, is not a cause of wonder; they are the only class of human beings with whom it ought to remain."‡ Let the advocates of slavery consider

* Singapore Chronicle, June 3, 1830.
† Par. Papers, 1838, pp. 90, 169, 306.
‡ Earle's Residence in New Zealand. Eclec. Rev., Sep. 1832.

with whom they are thus unceremoniously, but how justly, classed.

Of the Daerds, in *Canara,* under the Madras Presidency, the Collector of the Southern Division in 1801, states—"By far the greatest part of the slaves employed in agriculture are the Daerds, of whom there are various descriptions. No order was ever given for their being included in the registers; the whole number of them, by the population statement, is 52,022, men, women, and children.* Exclusive of the Daerds, there were another sect of slaves in Canara, though, I believe, many of them are now free. Under the Biddenore Government, all illegitimate children, save those by dancing girls, were considered the property of the Sircar, which sold them as slaves to any person who would purchase them; the number of this sort now is about 722; *there are also many slaves imported from Arabia.*"†

Some of the Daerds having enlisted in the Company's army, the Collector of *Mangalore* requested the Madras Government that they might be interdicted the service. The minute of Government acknowledges the existence of slavery in this and other parts of India.—"The circumstances stated by the Collector of the southern division of Canara, require, in the Board's opinion, particular consideration. He has represented, that serious injury will be sustained by the landholders of Canara, if their slaves are permitted to enter the sepoy corps, and desert the lands which they and their progenitors had cultivated for many generations. It is observed by Mr. Ravenshaw, that, where these people enlist, they seldom continue in the service, but almost invariably desert; in this point of view it appears ineligible that they should be allowed to enter the corps. As it may be considered beyond the province of the Board to discuss the propriety of this measure in a military point of view, or the policy of emancipating this class of people, they will only observe, that encouraging these slaves thus to desert their masters, would be *disturbing a property sanctioned to them by the usages of the country and the ordinances of their law.* Whilst it would be of no advantage to the army, *it would be of considerable detriment to the revenue; for not only in Canara, but in several parts of India, it is this class of people who cultivate the soil,* and on whose industry the landholder depends for the payment of the dues of the Sircar (government), and for the means of his own support."‡

* Par. Papers, 1828, p. 548. † 550. ‡ p. 552.

The Board of Revenue for the Madras Government in 1818, in a very judicious minute on slavery, candidly acknowledges its extensive prevalence:—

"The provinces now subject to this government, appear originally to have constituted several distinct Hindoo states, which are still to be traced by the difference of language, manners, and customs, that so strongly distinguish the inhabitants of one part of the country from the other. The five northern sircars of *Ganjam, Vizagapatam, Rajahmundry, Masulipatam,* and *Guntoor,* together with the districts of *Bellary, Cuddaph, Paluand,* and *Nellore,* or wherever the Telinga is the language of the people, may be considered one of these; the second may be said to include the district of *Chingleput,* the two divisions of the *Arcot Soobah, Salem, Baramahl, Coimbatore, Madura, Dindigul, Trichinopoly, Tanjore,* and *Tinnevelly,* or wherever the *Tamul* language is spoken; and the third comprises the provinces of *Malabar* and *Canara,* on the other coast of the Peninsula, where the Malayalam and Toolavo are the vernacular dialects of the country. *In all these districts, the labourer, who holds the plough, and performs the inferior offices of husbandry, is of the lowest, poorest, most ignorant, yet most numerous order in society; in general an outcast, or, at least, often of the degraded class of Hindoos, and usually resident in the outskirts of his village; everywhere without any property in the land which he can transfer by gift, sale, or bequest; and receiving from his employer, the ryot, little more than food, with a scanty supply of raiment!* It is almost superfluous to remark that, with this description of persons, the government officers have seldom had any direct communications; yet this may possibly be the cause that their situation has not yet received that consideration which it appears to merit. It is not, perhaps, sufficiently known, that throughout the Tamul country, as well as in Malabar and Canara, *the greater part of the labouring classes of the people have, from time immemorial, been in a state of acknowledged bondage, in which they continue to the present time.* It is, certainly, a curious circumstance, that in those provinces where the arbitrary system of the Mussulman government was established at the most early and for the longest period, where, consequently, the public assessment on the land is the highest, and private property in the soil the most rare and least valuable, the labourer should also be the most free; while his condition is the most abject, in those countries where the ancient institutions of the Hindoos have been the least disturbed, the public demand on the soil is the lightest, and private property in the land is universal and of the highest value. It seems probable, that slavery may have been as prevalent in the northern, as it now is in the southern and western provinces; and the same circumstances that reduced the landlord of Telingana to the situation of a landholder, may have tended gradually to weaken the power he possessed over his slaves, until they finally became emancipated from his authority."*

No correct idea can be formed from the Par. Papers of the number of slaves in British India. The slaves in *Batavia,* in 1812, before its surrender to the Dutch, exclusive of those belonging to Government, were—

At *Batavia* and its environs	18,972
Samarang division	4,488
Sourabaya division	3,682
	27,142†

* Par. Papers on Slavery in India, pp. 816, 817. † 1838, p. 157.

The following numbers have been ascertained from a careful examination of the Par. Papers of 1828 and 1838—

	Slaves.
*Canara, Malabar,** *Coorg, Wynaud, Cochin,* and *Travancore*	400,000†
Tinnevelley	324,000‡
Trichinopoly	10,600
Arcot, S. Division	3,000
—— N. Division	17,000
Southern Concan	2,000
Surat	2,000
Ceylon	27,397
Assam	11,300
Penang	3,000§
	800,297

The numerous extracts previously given, show that slavery very extensively prevails in many parts of India. The above items demonstrate that the number of slaves may equal and even far exceed that of the West Indies, at the time of their emancipation. And should not this fact be known, and efforts made to meliorate the state of these degraded people, and to elevate them to their proper place in society? When shall every subject of Britain be as free as the air he breathes? How tardy, though encouraged by success, are our proceedings in this work of justice and mercy. But this will more clearly appear in the following chapter.

CHAP. IV.

Methods proposed for the melioration and abolition of Slavery in India—Answers to objections to its abolition arising from the supposed kind treatment of slaves—The preservation of children and adults in famine by selling themselves for support—The indifference of the slaves to emancipation—Decreasing the population of an island or district—Mahomedan prejudices prohibiting any others than slaves attending on their women—and the interest of the slave-owners and the Government—Concluding appeal.

It is interesting to trace the various steps proposed or adopted for the melioration and abolition of slavery in India.

* Malabar alone 146,000. † Par. Papers, 1830, p. 211. ‡ 1838, p. 384. § p. 598.

The Madras Board of Revenue, in 1819, thus close their interesting letter, from which copious extracts have been given:—

"The Board are decidedly of opinion that slaves should not be sold for arrears of revenue; and prohibitory orders to this effect will be issued to Malabar, where alone it has occurred. In Malabar and Canara alone, the number of slaves is calculated at 180,000; and the Board have now under consideration certain propositions from Mr. Græme, the Commissioner in Mălabar, for the melioration of their condition, and the gradual emancipation of slaves in that country. In the Tamul provinces the number of slaves is comparatively few; their condition is better, and any immediate emancipation of them would be attended by inconvenience, difficulty, and perhaps distress. This might be at present deferred, until the practical remedy for the gradual abolition of slavery on the other coast shall have been fully considered and decided on. But, whatever may be the future decision respecting those who are already slaves, the Board think that a Regulation ought to be published, to prevent the further extension of slavery, and to meliorate, in some degree, by a few general enactments, the condition of those who are already slaves. The further purchase of free persons, as slaves, should be declared invalid and illegal; *and all children born slaves should be declared free.* But any person should be at liberty to contract, for a given sum, to labour for a term of years, or for life. Such contracts should be in writing, and only binding upon the individual who executes it, not upon his wife or children.

"Slaves should be declared competent *to possess and dispose of their own property,* to the exclusion of any interference on the part of their master. The Board further submit, whether it would not be proper to annex some penalty to the purchase of female children, for the purpose of being brought up as prostitutes. It might also be provided, that the proprietors are to provide wholesome food and clothing for their slaves; that in sickness, age, or infirmity, they shall not neglect them; that they shall not have the power of corporeal punishment; that slaves, on being ill-treated by their masters, shall be allowed to claim the privilege of being sold to another; and that in breach of these laws, or refusal to comply with them, on the part of the master, the slave shall receive his liberty. It might further be provided, *that slaves shall have the power to purchase their liberty at the price for which it was forfeited;* and that slaves attached to lands or estates, which may escheat to Government, shall be liberated. Many of these provisions will be found to contravene those of the Hindoo law, which, with respect to Hindoos, is declared by the regulations to be in force; and the necessity, therefore, of a formal enactment of them in the code will be sufficiently apparent. It may also be for the consideration of Government, whether the subject may not, as a general one, be referred, in the first instance, to the Supreme Government, in order to ascertain the state of slavery in the Bengal territories, and whether any restrictions are imposed on it."*

The propriety of improving the condition of slaves in India, has been urged by different functionaries of the British Government. Mr. Græme, in his Report on Malabar in 1822, made the following judicious remarks:—

"Upon occasion of the condition of the slaves of Malabar being brought into notice, it was lately suggested that slavery should be subjected to the rule of the Mahomedan law. This, if carried completely into effect, would indeed mitigate the severity of slavery, and render slaves in Malabar a very different race of

* Par. Papers on Slavery in India, 1828. p. 900.

mortals; but, strictly speaking, *slavery is not permitted by the Mahomedan law to be practised by any but Mussulmans, and even by them, only as regards the inhabitants of countries not agreeing to become converts to Mahomedanism, and at the same time refusing to pay the tax imposed by Mahomed upon infidels, or to permit the free exercise of the Mahomedan religion.* Slaves made so by stealth, and not in open war, or an authorized occasion, are not recognised by the Koran; and the acquisition of slaves by purchase, as practised by the Moplar Mahomedans in Malabar, is equally irreconcilable to the Mahomedan law. Ill-treatment of slaves is, with them, punishable by the slave being emancipated, or being sold to another master, on conviction before the quazee.

"Though it may be allowed that slavery in Malabar is not intolerable, and not exercised to an excessive degree of active cruelty, *the diminutive and squalid appearance, and the wretched hovels of a race of beings in the province*, who, by a census taken of the population in Fusly, 1216, (A. D. 1809) were reckoned to amount to 94,786, sufficiently indicate, *that they do not enjoy that comfortable state of existence which every person should have it in his power to acquire by his labour.* There are, no doubt, many freemen in the different ranks of society who are equally indigent with the slave. But among freemen there are many who are too proud, idle, and dishonest to work, and they have recourse to charity and fraudulent means to gain their subsistence; but it matters not, that many worthless characters are in worse circumstances; the question is—*whether slaves are as comfortable as they ought to be, and whether they acquire as much by their own industry in servitude, as they would in a free state.*"*

The Bengal consultations, as early as 1774, in a letter to the Council of *Dacca*, contain the following judicious and humane observations, respecting the annihilation of slavery.—"In those districts where slavery is in general usage, or any way connected with, or is likely to have any influence on the cultivation or revenue, which we are informed is the case at Sylhet, and may be so in the other (especially the frontier) parts of your division, we must desire you particularly to advise us what is the usage and every circumstance connected with it, and we shall then give such directions as we may judge to be necessary. Considering your reference, in the mean time, in the light of a general proposition, *we are of opinion, that the right of masters to the children of the slaves, already their property, cannot legally be taken from them in the* FIRST GENERATION; *but we think that this right cannot and ought not to extend further, and direct that you do make publication accordingly.*"†

It is to be deeply regretted that this excellent suggestion does not appear to have been acted upon. The second judge of the *Bareilly* Court of Circuit, in 1817, W. Leycester, Esq., proposed the same rational and effective method of gradually annihilating slavery. "Many estates in the country are cultivated by indigenous slaves, but it is very desirable it should no longer be possible to transfer the African slave-trade from the West to the East Indies, with only one proviso against it,

* Par. Papers on Slavery in India, 1828, p. 922. † p. 4.

that the slaves may not be resold; and it is also most desirable, that the present importation of females, for the purpose of breeding an hereditary race of slaves, should be put a stop to. *Nothing, perhaps, is so revolting as the idea of hereditary slavery*—of a man's inheriting, at his birth, nothing but the misfortunes of his parents, without hopes of emancipation, without the possibility of rising in life, through exertion or talent, and liable every moment to be taken to the market and sold, and transferred to the possession of another! I can hardly conceive that there could be any objection to modifying the present system of slavery, by an act declaring *the children of slaves to be free; that, if men will have slaves, they should also have to pay for them, and not to rear and inherit them like the produce of a farm-yard.*"* The reply of the Court of Nizamut Adawlut to this humane judge was as follows:—"The Court will only add, at present, that they participate in the sentiments expressed by Mr. Leycester, in abhorrence of hereditary slavery, and earnestly wish it could be discontinued, with regard to all children born under the British protection; but whilst it is allowed to remain, with respect to the progeny of existing slaves, born under the British Government in the West Indies and South Africa, the abolition of it, on general principles of justice and humanity, could not, the Court apprehend, be consistently proposed for India, where it has, from time immemorial, been sanctioned by the laws and usages of the country, and where the state of slavery is not so injurious to the objects of it, as in other countries where it is still maintained."† The recent abolition of slavery in these parts, may well form a powerful plea to extend the same boon to India.

The Madras Board of revenue, in 1818, express their conviction of the necessity and propriety of improving the civil condition of the slave;—

"The right which the slaves in the Tamul country possess to continue attached to the soil where they are born, which, though not universal, is pretty general among them; their dependence rather on a community than on an individual; and, perhaps, the vicinity of some of them to the Presidency, where a general knowledge prevails that the spirit of our government is inimical to bondage, seem all, more or less, to have contributed to render their condition in some degree superior to that of their brethren on the other coast. It is by no means, however,

* Par. Papers on Slavery in India, p. 345. "Domestic slavery, which is very common in India, however mild, demands the reprehension of every individual who has a proper idea of the dignity of human nature. In some parts of India children are as much an article of sale as goats or poultry."—Ward's *View of the Hindoos*, vol. iii. p. 281.

† Par. Papers, p. 346.

to be understood that this is universally the case. Their treatment necessarily depends principally on the individual character of their owners. *When we reflect on those evils that are inseparable from even the mildest state of slavery, and consider how large a portion of our most industrious subjects are at present totally deprived of a free market for their labour, restricted by inheritance to a mere subsistence, and sold and transferred with the land which they till,—policy, no less than humanity, would appear to dictate the propriety of gradually relieving them from those restrictions, which have reduced them, and must continue to confine them, to a condition scarcely superior to that of the cattle which they follow at the plough!*

"While such ought to be the policy pursued, with regard to this class of people, it would be obviously unjust to interfere with *the private property*, which there can be no doubt the ryots at present possess in their slaves; and it might be dangerous too suddenly to disturb the long established relations in society subsisting between these orders. For the present, it would seem sufficient *to define, by legislative enactments, the power which may be lawfully exercised by a ryot over his slaves*; but, as the revenue records do not afford information sufficiently minute and satisfactory for this purpose, it is resolved to call the particular attention of the collectors in Canara, Malabar, and the Tamul country, to this subject, and to desire that they will take an early opportunity to communicate fully their sentiments for the consideration of the Board."*

The Collector of the southern division of Arcot very judiciously remarks, upon these paragraphs;—"I take the liberty of suggesting that every labourer who is now free, shall be declared *exempt from all possibility of slavery;* denouncing penalties against every person who may attempt to enslave any subject under our government. Rules calculated to abolish the general abuse of slavery, to provide for slaves in sickness and old age, to confine the transfer of slaves to the village of their nativity, and to interdict all corporeal punishment or imprisonment, would prove an alleviation of the miseries inseparable from bondage. As the continuation, or the revival of slavery, is dependent upon the assistance owners contribute to the propagation of slaves, by advancing money for the expenses of marriages, a rule might be enacted, *prohibiting the enslaving of unborn children, by such a convention between the owners and their existing slaves.*"†

These extracts show some of the methods for the gradual melioration or abolition of slavery, contemplated by those whose opinions are given in the Parliamentary Documents. The philanthropist, who sighs, O! that all mankind were free! will rejoice to see a few proposals of more *immediate measures for the emancipation of slaves.* Upon "the practice of stealing children from their parents, and selling them for slaves," it is very justly remarked in a minute of the Governor-general in 1774,—"There appears no probable way of remedying this calamitous evil, but that of striking at the root of it, and

* Par. Papers on Slavery in India, p. 818. See also pp. 869—871.

† p. 872.

abolishing *the right of slavery*, excepting such cases to which the authority of Government cannot reach; such, as *laws in being have allowed, and where slaves have become a property by purchase, antecedent to the proposed prohibition.* The opinions of the most creditable of the Mussulman and Hindoo inhabitants, have been taken upon this subject, and they condemn the authorized usage of selling slaves, as repugnant to the particular precepts both of the Koran and the Shaster oppressive to the people, and injurious to the general welfare of the country." *

The Magistrates of *Patna*, in 1774, stated to the Governor general, Warren Hastings, Esq.;—" Whole families of slaves were formerly sold, but we do not find that the custom, though of old standing, and still in force, is now practised except in the mofussil, where sometimes the survivor of an old family, retired on his *altermga*, cultivates his lands by the hands of these slaves, who also perform the menial offices of the house. To a person thus situated, the keeping of slaves, may answer; the grain produced by their labour serving for their support. It seems that, on the sale of a slave who separately procures his own subsistence, only *one-half of the price is received by the owner, the other half going to the parents of the slave.* In the city, few people choose these Kahaar slaves, being indifferent to their business, and equally expensive with other servants. The female slaves are of more use in families, none being without them. It is urged, that a condition of this kind is consistent with the manners of a country where women are kept in continual retirement, and such privacy observed in regard to them as would be much affected by a frequent change of servants. *We do not imagine that alterations in the usage of slaves, will be attended with any consequences of moment to the cultivation or revenue of this province.*" †

In 1808, a Committee was appointed, by the Government of *Prince of Wales Island*, to report the state of slavery, and the propriety of its abolition. Three of the four European members expressed themselves as follows:—" After mature deliberation, the undersigned are of opinion, that the views of humanity, and of the British Legislature, signified in the late Acts respecting the abolition of slavery in the British West India Islands, may be extended and adopted here, consistently with due attention to the political circumstances of this settlement. And, with all deference, they beg leave to recommend

* Par. Papers on Slavery in India, 1828, p. 3.

† p. 5.

to the Honorable Board,—*the immediate and positive emancipation of slaves, in preference to relying on the accomplishment of it by the establishment of an annual tax, which, while the richer masters would be able to meet it, might have the effect only, to induce the poorer to insist with rigour and inhumanity, on greater exertions of service from their slaves, in order to enable them also to pay it.* Independent of the calls of humanity, and of the distinguished example afforded to the world by the British Legislature, the undersigned must allow that these considerations have also had much weight in inducing them to recommend the *immediate and positive emancipation of slaves;* though they at the same time are aware of the propriety and necessity of regarding, as far as is consistent with humanity, the *property* of the owner, and the prejudice of the natives of higher rank. These they are hopeful may be nearly assimilated by adopting, as the basis of emancipation, a custom which has been immemorially prevalent in the Malay countries, and on this island since the formation of the settlement, of *mortgaging labour in consideration of a sum advanced, for which the person or persons become debtor.*"*

The following was the late Governor Farquhar's plan for "annulling slavery in the shortest period in which that desirable object can be effected, without prejudice to individuals, or injury to the public interests in the settlement."—

"I recommend slavery being abolished at Prince of Wales Island. *It is the greatest of all evils, and the attempt to regulate such an evil is in itself almost absurd.* There was some excuse for using slaves in the West Indies, on account of the want of people, and Africa offered the readiest supply. But *there is no excuse for continuing the practice in India,—a country fully peopled, and where cultivation and commerce can be carried on by free men.* As slavery has in some degree been sanctioned by the government of Prince of Wales Island, it would be unjust, without an equivalent to the proprietors, to declare slaves free. Suppose that a committee were appointed to affix each slave, a value at which his master should be obliged to liberate him, on tender of the amount. Such as could not procure funds from their relations or friends, equal to the valuation, to become *debtors,* and serve the creditors, as now practised, under the following simple regulations :—The lender to find the borrower, in lieu of his services, meat, clothes, and lodging. If in chastising borrower for any fault (without the authority of the police) the lender bring blood, the debt to be cancelled. If the lender cohabit with any of the female borrowers, the debt to be cancelled. No idleness in the borrowers is to add to the debt; but, if dissatisfied, the lender may demand his money. Should the emancipated slave be unable to procure the money, the master may apply to the police, where the necessary inquiries will be made, and correction given accordingly. *The foregoing regulations would ameliorate the condition of those now slaves, and in time liberate the whole from debt, and give us from 4 to 5,000 good subjects in place of useless sufferers.* This is an object worthy of government's attention in every point of view."†

* Par. Papers on Slavery in India, 1828, pp. 440, 441. † pp. 434, 435.

"My own ideas," says W. E. Phillips, Esq., the successor of Governor Farquhar, in 1807, "are, that a committee should place a value on each slave, as also a value on his annual labour, after deducting his maintenance; and, that the slave should continue in bondage till the estimated value of his labour has reimbursed the master for his original cost. Should the slave deem himself ill treated, he may at any time sell the labour due to that master to one more mild, who may be disposed to advance that sum to the original master. As the value of labour here is very high, and that of slaves the reverse, I do not think I am sanguine in estimating, that *the greater part of these poor creatures would be free in* TWO YEARS, *from the date of their valuation.*" * †

In these sentiments the Hon. Court of Directors, in 1807, concurred. "As the toleration of slavery cannot be necessary at *Prince of Wales Island*, where the population is extensive and daily increasing, we consider it a subject deserving your serious notice, and direct that every means be resorted to for effecting its immediate abolition, provided the public interests of the settlement are not materially injured; but, even in that case, *we conceive an early period may be determined for the entire emancipation of slavery at your Presidency, from the date of which it ought by no means to be tolerated.*"‡ It is deeply to be regretted that these humane and judicious measures were not adopted. If they had been so, slavery might now have been unknown in this island.

F. Warden, Esq., member of Council, Bombay, thus unequivocally expressed his sentiments.—"Having gone so far towards the entire abolition of the trade and sale of slaves, I do not apprehend creating the slightest danger or alarm in giving effect to the original proposition of the Governor. I presume not to sketch the *mode*, or to fix the *period* of general emancipation, and, perhaps, the sudden manumission of those now actually in a state of bondage, though abstractedly just

* Par. Papers on Slavery in India, 1828, p. 436. ‡ p. 435.

† This judicious plan was adopted at *Singapore*, by Sir Stamford Raffles. "Slavery was abolishe din the settlement, with the reservation of what were called *slave debtors*,—persons who had engaged their services in payment of debt duly incurred. These were protected by having all their civil privileges preserved to them, excepting only the freedom of service. They were not allowed to be transferred to other masters, without their own consent; if their creditors died solvent they were discharged forthwith; if insolvent they were allowed to choose a master, and the value of their labour was carried to the bankrupt estate; but in no case could they be thus pledged, or kept for a longer period than *five years*, nor for a less sum than *twenty dollars yearly*."—Mem. of Sir S. Raffles. *Ori. Quar. Rev., April* 1830, p. 488.

might not be politically wise; but, there can exist no reason, either political or humane, against the British government *prohibiting the purchase or sale of slaves, legitimate or illegitimate, after a specified time, and likewise ordaining and declaring that all children born of parents in a state of slavery, shall from a like date be free.*'"* In 1818, J. H. Harrington, Esq., member of Council in Calcutta, prepared a regulation to be submitted to the British government for the abolition of slavery. He was favourable to the idea of *fixing a period from which all that are born in a state of slavery shall be free.* The letter and the proposed regulation are lengthened, weighty, and valuable documents. See Par. Papers, 1838. pp. 315—326. How lamentable that so little is done in this work of justice and mercy, for the degraded ranks of our fellow subjects in British India!

It may be presumed, that *various objections to the extensive melioration, and particularly the abolition of slavery, exist among the advocates of the slave system in India.* It will now be our object, from the documents already adverted to, to notice the principal of these objections, and to obviate them —not with our own arguments or language, but that of gentlemen in India, intimately acquainted with the subject upon which they have written. The official nature of these replies must add considerably to their value.

One of the most common objections to the discontinuance of the present system of slavery, in British India, is—*the supposed kind treatment of the slaves.* The presumed mild nature of East India slavery, is often used as a reason for its continuance, and its abolition denounced as an evil. To this argument for slavery, the following extract from the Madras Board of Revenue, affords an appropriate reply.

"Because no immediate measures are urgently called for, it does not follow, that—*the most useful, the most laborious, and one of the most numerous classes of our subjects in these territories, should, from generation to generation, continue the hereditary bondsmen of their masters,—incapable of inheriting property of their own,—deprived of that stimulus to industry which possession of property ever inspires; and, because they are fed, clothed, and reconciled to their present condition, it does not follow that the Government should confirm institutions which doom those who have thus fallen into this condition, incapable of ever recovering their liberty, or of rising to a level with their fellow men!* Independently of those principles, hostile to any restraint on liberty, which are innate in every British government, and which, as contained in our judicial code, without any express enactment on the subject, have operated to check abuses of masters towards their slaves; and, independently also of those feelings, among free men, which naturally prompt them to extend to every one under their government the blessings which freedom confers, it appears

* Par. Papers, 1838, pp. 324, 404.

to the Board, on the mere calculating principle of self interest and policy, to be desirable that no one should be deprived of the means of acquiring property, or of diffusing those benefits among society which proceed from an increase of capital and wealth."*

"The general opinion," says Mr. Warder, member of council in Bombay, 1826, "that prevails in support of slavery, that it is so leniently conducted, as to weaken the objections arising from the principle, is precisely of the same nature as the arguments that have been invariably used by the advocates of the Slave trade; *a principle that is in its nature inhuman and abhorrent, can, in my estimation, derive support from such an argument*."†

A second reason urged for the perpetuation of slavery, and consequently an objection to its abolition, is the *preservation of children and adults in famine, by being sold for support.* On this view of the subject, which it must be confessed is one of considerable delicacy and importance, several Indian magistrates have given their opinion. The magistrate of *Tiperah*, under the Bengal Presidency, in 1816, writes—"Report states that, in the Mogul government, slavery existed in the district of *Sylhet* to such a degree, that persons would sell themselves as slaves to satisfy demands of rent; while others would, from similar necessity, dispose of their own slaves. Even at the present day it may be ascertained that some individuals, in order to supply the immediate wants of nature, voluntarily submit to a state of slavery, and dispose of their persons for determinate services, so long as they may be capable of performing them. Documents to this effect are executed in the customary manner with other written engagements; and the court may easily obtain them from the magistrate of Sylhet. Since necessity alone would compel any person to submit to a state of slavery, it may, I presume, be inferred, that the slavery herein noticed originates in the extreme poverty of the lower orders of society, and to tolerate it, under certain restrictions, would be preferable to exposing the poorer classes of the community to the risk of perishing for want, by depriving them of the only ostensible resource left to enable them to support existence."‡

Relative to this state of things, it is judiciously observed, by W. Leycester, Esq., the second judge of *Bareilly*—"I know it is argued, that slaves in India are treated kindly;

* Par. Papers on Slavery in India, 1828, p. 899. 1838, p. 314. † p. 457.
‡ p. 24.

that they are comfortable; that in times of scarcity many must starve and die, if people who have the means of feeding them are not allowed to purchase them as slaves. Many, I believe, are treated kindly; but that all are so, that there is not a great deal of ill treatment, nobody will, I believe, assert; and there is not a crime committed among mankind that has not, at one time or other, produced an incidental good, and it would be strange indeed if slavery were the only exception. But, it might be considered an adequate inducement to deeds of charity, to compensate them by the labours of the object of it, *during one generation, instead of aggravating the sorrows of accidental necessity by slavery through all generations.*"*

The second judge of *Moorshedabad* in 1814, and the magistrate of *Tanjore* in 1825, recommend that in seasons of great distress from famine, it should be allowed to sell children for a *limited period.* The latter gentleman says—"In seasons of great scarcity and distress it would perhaps be driving parents to great extremities, and more abhorrent to human nature, were any penalty attached to the sale of children by their own parents, or to the purchase of them direct from their parents; but the traffic should, in my opinion, be most strictly prohibited from extending any further, and a *person, purchasing a child from its parents, should on no account have the power of disposing of it to another.*"†

A third objection to the suppression of slavery in India is *the supposed indifference of the slaves to their emancipation.* The collector of the southern division of *Canara,* in 1801, in describing the condition of the Daerds, advocates this sentiment:—

"Slavery has been defined, 'an obligation to labour for the benefit of the master, without the contract or consent of the servant, the master at the same time having the right to dispose of him by sale, or in any other way to make him the property of a third person.' The sect of the Daerds who are bought and sold, and who come nearest to the description of slaves, differ from them in the following respects: first, their service is *conditional;* a master, at the time of purchase, agrees to give them the usual allowance of rice, cloth, &c.; if he fails, and refuses to do this, the Daerds are no longer bound to serve him, and can recover the balance of allowance due to them and their children. If the purchaser agrees to give the established allowances, the Daerds cannot refuse to enter his service; but if, from any real cause, they have a dread of their man, the old master will generally, on being asked, keep them until he can get another purchaser. A master cannot make a traffic of them, that is, he cannot put them

* Par. Papers on Slavery in India, 1828, p. 345. See also pp. 300, 325, 484.

† p. 930. See also p. 325.

up to public sale, or transport them, either by sea or land, to any place where there are not people of their own cast, which is confined to Canara; they can never be sent out of the province; they can even refuse to be sold out of the manganny in which they are born. This sect, and their children, may be called '*conditional servants for ever*.' Those of the maurey Daerds, who are attached to estates, have the same privilege as those just mentioned, except that, in case of their landlord omitting to give them their regular allowance of rice, &c., they cannot quit his lands; but on making a complaint, they can recover their right, with damages. All other descriptions of Daerds are '*conditional servants on the male side for life;*' and in no case have they, so long as their master feeds and clothes them according to usage, a right to leave his service. Slavery is objected to, as being contrary to the fundamental principles of morality, because both men and women in that state, it is said, are tempted to commit and excite others to crimes they would not do in a free state. Supposing that the service of the Daerds could be construed slavery, which in my opinion it cannot, the same objection does not apply to it, because, with them, it is merely the custom of their cast; and they are in general more attached to their wives and families, who live with them, than most other sects."*

The interest of the slave proprietors, and not that of the slaves, is the great question in these remarks. But who can doubt whether slavery be better than freedom? The records of slavery, whether eastern or western, afford abundant proof of the dissatisfaction, poverty, and misery attendant upon slavery, and consequently, the desire of the slave to be free. The following additional extract may suffice:—"It is a question," says M. Elphinstone, Esq., Resident at *Poona*, in 1817, "how we are to treat slaves, subjects of his Highness the Paishwa, who fly from their masters, also subjects of his Highness, and take refuge in our camps. It is so obvious, that *we cannot open an asylum for fugitive slaves* within the Paishwa's territories, that I have hitherto directed persons in these circumstances to be refused leave to reside in our camps; but I shall be happy to be informed what is the proper course in such cases, and generally what is the law relative to the traffic in slaves, as far as is applicable to our forces in the territories of allied princes."†—That slaves generally are indifferent to freedom—to the acquisition of property—to elevation in society—will rarely be received by those at all acquainted with that system, which, to use the words of Earl Minto, "must be viewed as a violation of one of the first principles on which society is constituted."‡

Another objection to the abolition of slavery occurs in the Papers relative to Prince of Wales Island, viz. *decreasing the population.*§ There might be some appearance of pro-

* Par. Papers on Slavery in India, pp. 550, 551.
† p. 332. ‡ p. 172. § p. 440.

priety in this remark, as it respected the resort to the Island of Malays, Mahomedans, Chinese, and other nations who are favourable to slavery; but few of the advocates of slavery can be insensible, that this system is inimical to the increase of population, and that its gains are "the price of blood."—"The great advantage to population (says the judge of Bundlecund in 1808), derived from the emancipation of slaves, cannot be better illustrated than by quoting an example adduced by Mr. Coxe, in his tour through the northern countries of Europe. Speaking of the slavery of the Polish peasantry, he has the following remarkable instance of the benefit accruing from their manumission. A few nobles, of benevolent hearts, 'and enlightened understandings, ventured upon the expediency of giving liberty to their vassals. The event has shown this project to be no less judicious than humane; no less friendly to their own interests than the happiness of their peasants. For it appears that, in the districts in which the new arrangement has been introduced, the population of the villages has been considerably increased, and the revenues of their estates augmented in a triple proportion.' The first nobleman who granted freedom to his peasants was Zamoiske, formerly great chancellor, who, in 1760, enfranchised six villages in the palatinate of Moravia. These villages were, in 1777, visited by the author of *The Patriotic Letters.* On inspecting the parish registers of births from 1750 to 1760, during the last ten years of slavery immediately preceding their enfranchisement, he found the number of births 434; in the first ten years of their freedom, from 1760 to 1770, 620; and from 1770 to the beginning of 1777, 585 births. If we suppose an improvement of this sort to take place, throughout the kingdom, how great would be the increase of population!"* The argument against slavery arising from its depopulating tendency, is unanswerable.†

* Par Papers, 1828, p. 301.

† "Upon the authority of *Cape Papers,* in Dec. 1828, the slave population is found, from recent enumeration, to have been nearly stationary (in the Cape Colony) from 30 to 35,000, during the last *twenty* years; although in that period, the *free* population of all classes and colours has almost doubled itself. The deplorable statistics of our West India Islands, where the slave population, as the registry proves, actually *decreased* 28,000 *in six years!* leaves us little to be surprised on this score."—Eclec. Rev. Jan. 1831, p. 37. "The awful mortality," says Mr. Scoble, "which has prevailed in all the West Indian Islands (with one exception) is almost incredible. In eleven years the actual decrease of the population, over and above the births, was more than

An objection to the abolition of slavery peculiar to the Mahomedans is made on the ground, that the injunctions of their Prophet, prohibit *any other than slaves attending on their women, and that they cannot dispense with slaves.* The nature of this objection, and the reply to it, are stated in the communication of the European members of the committee formed at Prince of Wales Island, in 1808, to consider the propriety of the suppression of slavery in the island.—" In support of this opinion (say the committee), they adduce a passage in their Koran, which, on reference to Sale's translation of it,* the committee find translated thus :—' And speak unto the believing women, that they restrain their eyes and preserve their modesty, and discover not their ornaments, except what necessarily appeareth ; and let them throw their veils over their bosoms, and not show their ornaments unless to their husbands, or their fathers, or their husband's fathers, or their sons, or their husband's sons, or their brothers, or their brothers' sons, or their sisters' sons, or their women, or the captives which their right hand may possess, or unto such men as attend them and have no need of women, or unto children who distinguish not the nakedness of women; and let them not make a noise with their feet, that their ornaments which they hide may thereby be discovered.' The undersigned deem it unnecessary to state to the honourable board the import, in their opinion, of this passage, or to elucidate it by remarking how much the manners of the Mahomedan society, particularly of the poorer classes, are in opposition to the doctrine deduced from it. They beg leave to call the attention of the board to the following passage only of the Koran:—' And unto such of your slaves as desire a written instrument allowing them to redeem themselves on paying a certain sum, write one, if you know good in them, and give them of the riches of God, which he hath given you.'† Which certainly not only directly enjoins the emancipation of slaves, but exactly in the manner suggested by the undersigned members. They, however, are far from wishing to recommend the adoption of any measure which might be generally disagreeable to the Mahomedan commu-

32,000, in a population of 800,000. This mortality occasioned by over working, was not less during the apprenticeship ; for the planters knowing that the existence of slavery was limited, were induced to extort as much labour from the slaves as possible while in their power. Many of them by over-working, were to use a familiar expression almost " used up," and entered the state of freedom nearly exhausted? *Chronicle*, 1839.

* Vol. ii .p. 192. † Sale's Translation, vol. ii. p. 194.

nity, whether their objections to it originate in ignorant prejudice, or from a regard to interest and convenience; but they have good reason to believe that the opposition, even among the followers of the Mahomedan religion, to the emancipation of slaves, is very partial, and confined almost entirely to a few of the first rank."*

The Mahomedans state on the general principle of this objection to the emancipation of slaves (to use the language of the European member of the committee who, with the native members of it, dissented from his brethren): "By the law of their prophet, a Mussulman may have four wives, if he can afford to maintain so many, and he is not restricted to *any number of concubines.* His wives are generally chosen among the daughters of free men of equal rank with himself, but his concubines can only be taken from among his slaves. Now, say they, if all slaves are emancipated, or made simple debtors, our concubines will of course have it in their power to leave us, on paying the sum fixed upon as their value, which in most instances they will be able to do, from the fruits of their master's generosity; and, in this infant and confined settlement, Mahomedans will find it difficult to meet with suitable wives. It is considered by all Mahomedans, but particularly among the higher classes of Malays, a very great disgrace for a woman, with whom he he has once lived, to go with strange men, or leave his house without his consent, which their emancipation will enable them to do, even while they are with child by their master."† The precept of the Koran enjoins giving slaves "a written instrument, allowing them to redeem themselves on paying a certain sum." Why oppose the abolition of slavery with such a precept before them? Is it not evidently from other motives than those of respect to their religion?

But the principal objection to the abolition of slavery, is that which arises from *the interest of the slave owners, and of the government.* On this view of the subject it is stated by W. B. Bayley, Esq., Secretary to the Bengal Government in 1817,—"With reference to the extent to which domestic slavery exists in India, under the established laws and usages of the Hindoos and Mahomedans, and to the known habits and feelings of the people relative to that point, the Vice-President in council is of opinion, that the greatest care should be observed to guard against the prevalence of an im-

* Par. Papers, p. 445; see also Par. Papers, 1838, p. 606.
† p. 444.

pression, amongst the natives, that any general or direct interference, in the existing relation of master and slave, is contemplated by Government. Any impression of that nature might be expected to excite feelings of alarm and dissatisfaction; and on this ground it appears to be of importance that the Government of Bombay should avoid, as far as may be practicable, the official revival and discussion of this question, after the deliberate consideration which it has undergone in communication with the legal authorities at this Presidency."* In 1826 the same sentiments were expressed by the Govenor-general. "I find no statement of existing evils which render it incumbent on the government to enter into the consideration of the state of slavery in India; under the absence of all complaint, and the apparent want of any pressing necessity for inquiry, I think it would be inexpedient to hazard the inconvenience of a precipitate agitation of the question."† Surely a brighter day is now dawning upon the myriads of slaves in India.

The collector of Trichinopoly, in 1818, gives his views upon the difficulty of the question of the abolition of slavery in the following terms:—

"I shall submit my opinion, as to the policy of abolishing this establishment. There is something so revolting to an Englishman, in the idea of slavery, that the advocates for its continuance *in any shape* must ever labour under the disadvantage of pre-judgment. Notwithstanding this, I shall endeavour to show that, so far as relates to *the revenue of this district* (and I trust my opinion will not be supposed to extend further), the abolition of the puller system would be attended with the most ruinous consequences. It has been the custom, to describe the pullers as the lowest order of society, involved in wretchedness and misery, and reduced to a condition 'scarcely superior to that of the cattle which they follow at the plough.' *In Malabar, it would also appear, that the human form has even changed its wonted appearance, and that the slaves are distinguishable by their diminutiveness!* This theme holds out a fine subject for declamation; but, so far as it relates to this class of people in Trichinopoly, it is highly erroneous, inasmuch as there is no class of people generally so athletic or tall as the pullers. It may be urged, *that there is something degrading in a government being concerned, in selling human beings, 'like so many cattle.'* It would, perhaps, be better if it could be avoided; but so long as the land continues possessed by Brahmun meerassidars, who, by the immutable laws of cast, are prevented personally exercising the offices of agriculture, I see no possible means of collecting the revenue, nor of cultivating the land, without the establishment of pullers (slaves). Divesting the discussion of national feeling, the most obvious inconveniences and evil which attend it are—that a man, for the sake of food and other necessaries of life, is condemned to perpetual labour. I exclude all unreasonable rigour on the part of the master, because I have already shown that the ruling principle of human conduct, self interest, is conducive, in the present instance, to soften severity. But whether this obligation to perpetual labour, on the part of the puller, is not fully requited by a perpetual certainty of maintenance (for which those who work for hire are often at a loss) may, I think, be fairly

* Par. Papers, 1828, p. 335 † 1838, pp. 328, 329.

doubted. It is, however, possible, that the advocates of freedom may think with Cicero, and the third judge in Malabar, '*Mihi liber esse non videtur, qui non aliquando nihil agit.*' *

To these remarks, it is presumed the report of Mr. Græme on *Malabar*, in 1822, furnishes a very satisfactory reply.—

"The most serious objections, I have heard, against any active measure in favour of the slaves of Malabar, are *the violation of the rights of private property which it would involve*, the necessity to which the proprietors would be subjected of paying more for labour, employed in the cultivation of their lands, and the difficulty which slaves would have of subsisting, if left to their own resources. It is not requisite to make such an abrupt innovation, upon established rites and customs, as to declare the slaves to be free forthwith; but, *a prospect should be opened of eventual but gradual emancipation, and proprietors should be indemnified by the payment of a maximum price, which should previously be ascertained for each district, and promulgated.* To set the example, Government might be disposed to sanction the occasional appropriation of small sums annually to the purchase of slaves, and to accept slaves in payment of arrears of revenue, which from being too heavy, it might, at all events be advisable to remit; but, in all these cases, the wishes of the individuals themselves should be consulted, and they should not be emancipated, unless they feel confident of being able to earn their own livelihood without assistance. Slaves should also have the power of redeeming themselves from servitude, whenever the exertions of their own industry may place them in a state of indemnifying their masters for the loss of their rights of property over them. The magistrate should have the power of fining or emancipating for ill treatment. It need not be apprehended that these provisions would bring about an emancipation too rapidly; but the knowledge of their future operation would, in the mean time, *act as a stimulus to the activity of the slaves, and it would insure better treatment on the part of the proprietors.* Slaves, thus cautiously emancipated, would not be likely to leave their usual places of residence as long as they afforded the necessary means of subsistence: and that in most cases they would, there can be little doubt; for there could be nothing to diminish the demand of their old masters for their services. They would therefore still be living on the old estates, but more comfortably and probably less addicted to the petty pilfering of which their masters now accuse them. A great improvement might be expected to take place in the state of cultivation in the province. Not only would the old slaves work more cheerfully, and with more effect, but many proprietors in the southern division, who from indolence leave every thing to their slaves, would be inclined to betake themselves to manual labour, when they found that they were obliged to pay higher for it in others. Upon the principles of these observations, I have drawn out a Regulation respecting slaves, which I have submitted to Government through the Board of Revenue. The cautious nature of the different provisions renders it easy to apply it to *Canara* as well as *Malabar*, without inconvenience; for, though in *Canara* slavery may be considered to exist in a milder form, its gradual supercession would be attended with benefit.†

More particular information is requisite on the subject of slavery in India, relative to the actual number of slaves; 'the relations of master and slave;' the nature of their employment, provision, increase, or decrease, &c.

* Par. Papers, Slavery in India, 1828, p. 893, 894. † p. 923.

Though the Par. Papers, 1828, contain 418 folio pages respecting slavery in the Bengal Presidency, not a single item appears which may furnish data on which to ascertain the number of slaves in that part of India. This must be considered a serious defect. The same remark applies to the Presidency of Bombay; and as it respects Madras, with a few exceptions supplied by the Collectors, but little information can be procured of the actual number of slaves. The want of laws, to regulate the conduct of the owners of slaves, appears a very great evil in East Indian slavery. What can justify such sentiments as the following:—"We desire that you will be extremely cautious in making any regulation for defining the relations of master and slave. It is our wish to improve the condition of the latter to the utmost extent, and we fear that, in defining the power of masters, acts of compulsion might be legalized, which by custom are not now tolerated, and the slaves might be placed in a worse condition than before."* Is uncertain custom better than law? How can the treatment of the slave be known, while there are no written published laws to which he can appeal? Is not this procedure calculated to keep the degraded slave *in statu quo?* From the Madras papers some idea may be formed of the nature of the employment of slaves, and the provision allowed them; but more full information is desirable.

Whether *the slave population in India increases or decreases does not appear*. The destructive influence of slavery in some of the West Indian Islands has been most appalling. "Into Jamaica alone, since the conquest (in 1665), when there were in it about 40,000 slaves, not less than 850,000 Africans have been imported; making a total of 890,000, exclusive of all the births which have taken place during that period. And yet, at the present moment, the slave population of the island does not exceed 345,000! No fewer than 545,000 slaves more than now exist there have been imported into this single island! It is for Jamaica to account for so great a waste of life."† G. A. Carruthers, Esq., in evidence before a Committee of the Lords, in 1830, declared—"On no plantation in *Brazil* do the slave population keep up their numbers. I do not know whether they will now; but the masters went on the principle of neglecting their slaves, and supplying themselves at a very cheap rate: I have known them sold at £20 each."‡ It may be presumed that slavery in the East is not

* Par. Papers on Slavery in India, 1828, p. 901.
† East and West India Sugar (Hatchard), p. 34. ‡ Par. Papers, 1830, p. 322.

so prejudicial to the increase, civilization, and happiness of the human race, as it has been in the West; but more particular information is necessary to form a correct judgment of its real nature and influence.*

It is the duty of Britain to meliorate and abolish slavery in every part of her dominions. Slavery in the East may be greatly mitigated by the benign influence of the British Government; and the Madras Board of Revenue, in 1819, suggested, "that the further purchase of free persons as slaves should be declared invalid and illegal, and *all children hereafter born slaves should be free;* that however any person might contract, in writing, for a term of years or for life, such contract should be binding only upon the individual who executes it. That slaves should be held competent to possess property, and to dispose of it, without their masters' interference; that the purchase of female children, to be educated as prostitutes, should be prohibited: that owners of slaves should be bound to provide wholesome food for them, as well as clothing, and not to neglect them in sickness, age, or infirmity; that they should be deprived of the power of corporeal punishment: that slaves, ill-treated by their masters, should be allowed to change owners; that a breach of the law should enfranchise the slave; *that slaves should be allowed to purchase their liberty at the price paid for it;* and that slaves attached to lands which may escheat to Government should be liberated."† Why is Britain so timid, so tardy, in conferring upon her Asiatic subjects the blessings of freedom? It is important that the state of slavery in India should be more fully and generally known, and the practicability and utility of its entire suppression pressed upon the attention of the Legislature.‡

* "The sin of blood," says Dr. South, "is a destroying, wasting, murdering sin, murdering others besides those whom it kills. It breaks the back of Governments, sinks families, destroys for the future, reaches into successions, and cuts off posterities."

† Asi. Jour., Jan. 1829, p. 30. Par. Papers, p. 900.

‡ "Sir Thomas Smith (Secretary to Edward VI.) testifies, that he never knew any *villain in gross*, throughout the realm, and the few *villains regardant* remaining, were such only as belonged to bishops, monasteries, or other ecclesiastical corporations, in the preceding times of Popery. His words are, 'The holy fathers, monks, and friars, had at their confessions, and specially in their extreme and deadly sickness, convinced the laity how dangerous a practice it was *for one Christian man to hold another in bondage:* so that temporal men, by little and little, by reason of that horror in their consciences, were glad to manumit all their villains. But the said holy fathers, with the abbots and priors, *did not in like sort by theirs.* They had a scruple in conscience to impoverish and de-

The adoption and encouragement of free labour are of great importance in promoting the abolition of slavery. Its utility in the cultivation of *indigo* in India is very apparent. The first few chests arrived in England in 1787: it is now estimated to employ nearly 500,000 free persons, and the article has ceased to be cultivated by slaves. "It is not known that there is any indigo whatever cultivated by slave labour, although, from the nature of things, it may be difficult to ascertain it with certainty; the quantity, however, if any, must be exceedingly small."* It is a question of much interest—*Is East India sugar the product of slave labour or not?* This has been asserted by some writers, and as positively denied by others. It is evident, from the Papers on Eastern Slavery, that the greatest number of slaves is found on the Malabar coast. No sugars are exported from Malabar, but it is stated, that sugar is imported for home consumption. In Bengal, a great sugar province of India, the number of slaves, compared with other parts of Hindostan, appears comparatively small. "In this country," says the Bengal Board of Trade, in 1792, "the cultivator is either the immediate proprietor of the ground, or he hires it, as in Europe, of the proprietor; and uses his discretion in cultivating what he thinks best adapted to the nature of the soil, or the demand of the market. One field produces sugar, the next wheat, rice, or cotton. The Bengal peasantry are freemen, and are, in the usual course of nature, replaced by their children. The Bengal peasant is actuated by the ordinary wants and desires of mankind. His family assist his labour and soothe his toil, and the sharp eye of personal interest guides his judgment. In the West Indies, the whole labour of the ground is performed by hand, with the spade or hoe. Here the ox and plough, as in Europe, lessen the labour of man, and facilitate the productions of the earth."† Slave labour is not an item in the different estimates given of the price of cultivating sugar. Mr. Udney, resident at Malda, in 1793, writes, "The expense of cultivating one bigah (about 1,600 square feet) is estimated at 8ru. 8an. whereof the particulars are,

spoil the church so much, as to manumit such as were bound to their churches, or to the manors which the church had gotten; and so kept their villains still.' By the statute of Charles II. the tenure in villainage was virtually abolished, and at that time there was hardly a pure villain (or slave) left in the nation."—*Blackstone's* Com. vol. ii. p. 96.

* See "A short Review of the Slave Trade," &c., Birmingham, 1827.

† "Papers respecting the cultivation and manufacture of sugar in British India." 1822, pp. 53, 60, 146. See also pp. 32, 92, &c.

	ru.	an.
Hire of Ploughs, oxen, &c.	1	12
Cooley (labourers) hire	0	14
Do. weeding eight times	4	0
Do. cutting and bringing earth	0	8
Do. tying canes four times	1	0
Petty charges	0	6
	8	8."*

"But we may spare ourselves the trouble (says the Anti-Slavery Reporter, for Sep. 1829), of confuting the elaborate misstatements of our adversaries on this question. The controversy is fast tending to its termination. The march of events will scarcely leave room, much longer, either for misrepresentation or misapprehension. The facilities already given in Bengal, by Lord W. Bentinck, to the investment of British capital, and the development of British skill in the cultivation of the soil; the almost certainty that those fiscal regulations which have hitherto depressed the growth of sugar in Bengal, and prevented the large increase of its imports into this country, will soon be repealed; the prospect of an early removal of the other restrictions, which still fetter the commerce of our Eastern possessions; the rapidly increasing population and prosperity of Hayti; the official statements of Mr. Ward, as to the profitable culture of sugar by free labour in Mexico; and the rapid extension of the manufacture of beet-root sugar in France (a prelude, as we conceive, to its introduction into this country, and especially into Ireland); all these circumstances, combined, afford a promise which can scarcely fail of seeing a death blow inflicted on the culture of sugar by slave labour."

Much encouragement may be derived, as it respects the abolition of slavery in British India, from the just and humane sentiments on the subject, frequently expressed by the functionaries of the Indian government,—from the extent of our power,—and the general abhorrence in which slavery is held in Britain.

The author, while arranging the contents of the voluminous Papers on East India Slavery, noticed some of the excellent

* For an ample investigation of this question, see "A Letter to W. W. Whitmore, Esq., M. P., in reply to the erroneous statements of the late J. Marryat, Esq., on the subject of slavery in the East Indies." Hatchard, 1823. Ori. Herald., Oct. 1829. The Anti-slavery Reporter, Sep. 1829. East India Slavery, by G. Saintsbury, Tilt, Fleet Street, &c.

sentiments of the authorities in India relative to the nature and injurious tendency of slavery; they are as follow,—

"I make no scruple to declare my opinion, that absolute unconditional slavery, by which one human creature becomes the property of another, like a horse or an ox, is happily unknown to the law of England; and that no human law could give it a just sanction."*—Sir W. Jones.

"It is impossible to think, without horror, of whole generations being born to slavery."†—T. C. Metcalfe, Esq., Resident at Delhi, now Governor of Jamaica.

"The British retain the rights of their birth, and ought also to retain all the relations connected with the British character—to which, it is equally abhorrent to be the master of slaves, as to endure slavery."‡—W. Thackery, Esq., Chief Secretary to Government, Calcutta.

"Slavery is always liable to be attended with the greatest abuse; which, however mild and unobjectionable it may sometimes be in its application, must still be viewed as a violation of one of the first principles on which society is constituted."§—Lord Minto.

"Slavery under any shape, or if it bears only the name, is so repugnant to every principle of enlightened administration, and so inconsistent with your Lordship's benevolent plans, that I fear I should not stand excused in my defence of such a system, under any modifications or circumstances whatever."‖—Sir Stamford Raffles.

"Slavery is the greatest of all evils; and the attempt to regulate such an evil is in itself almost absurd. There is no excuse for continuing the practice in India, a country fully peopled, and where cultivation and commerce can be carried on by free men."¶—Governor Farquhar.

"Slavery in its mildest forms is degrading to the minds of Britons."**—W. E. Philips, Esq., Governor of Prince of Wales Island.

"Nothing, perhaps, is so revolting as the idea of hereditary slavery. It might be considered an adequate inducement to deeds of charity, to compensate them by the labours of the object of it during one generation, instead of aggravating the sorrows of accidental necessity, by slavery through all generations."††—W. Leycester, Esq., Judge of Bareilly.

"Slavery in every form is an evil of great magnitude, and peculiarly revolting to the moral feelings of Englishmen."‡‡—J. Loch, Esq.

"A practice so dissonant to the British government, and so revolting to the feelings of humanity."§§

"I do not conceive that the *unsophisticated* administration of British law, unmodified by Act of Parliament, can tolerate the existence of slavery."‖‖—S. Garling, Esq.

"The Hon. the Governor cannot but avail himself of this opportunity of impressing on your minds the extreme repugnance of the British principles of government towards the state of slavery."¶¶—J. Patullo, Esq., Secretary to Malacca government.

"Slavery violates fundamental principles. The inviolability of property rests upon original free occupancy of that which rightfully belonged to no other person at the period of occupancy. The laws which regulate slavery are exceptions to the general principles of our national code; however expedient or necessary they may be esteemed, they set at naught that which men enjoying the pure sanctions of English law consider their indefeasible birthright."***—S. Garling.

"The Hindoos may claim all toleration for their religious ordinances, but none for the vices of their civil policy, when out of two equal men it would constitute

* Par. Papers on Slavery in India, 1828, p. 9. † p. 105. ‡ p. 147. § p. 172. ‖ p. 157. See pp. 303, 317. ¶ p. 434. ** p. 425. †† p. 345. ‡‡ 1838, p. 2. §§ p. 24. ‖‖ pp. 216, 264. ¶¶ p. 260. *** p. 265

one the slave to the other, and degrade both; making the slave master little better than a brute, and reducing the slave to the level of an instinctive animal. The *antiquity* of the iniquity has nothing to do with the question. It first visited the world as a curse, and as long as it continues we may feel assured it will continue a curse."*—Judge Leycester.

"It is obviously repugnant to every principle of natural justice, and inconsistent with the common rights of mankind, that any person should be deprived of his personal freedom during the whole of life, without his consent, and without having committed any offence subject to so heavy a punishment."†—J. H. Harington, Esq.

"I have always looked upon the mere tolerance of slavery as unjust in itself, and consequently I can have no hesitation in giving my opinion that its abolition may take place without violating justice."‡—T. Brodie, Esq.

"In Macnaghten's book of Mahomedan law, the sale of children is declared illegal."§

Let such sentiments as these become general among those who hold in their hands the destinies of India, and it may be justly anticipated, that slavery at no very distant period will be annihilated.‖

The influence of the British Government in India is great, and may be safely and successfully exerted in abolishing slavery and every inhuman custom. It was justly remarked, by the late Bishop Heber, that in India, "our will is our law." Let Britain sincerely will the good of India, and what may not be accomplished? To use the language of Mr. Græme's Report on Malabar, in 1822,—"It matters not that many worthless characters are in worse circumstances than the slave; the question is—*whether slaves are as comfortable as they ought to be, and whether they acquire as much by their own industry, in servitude, as they would in a free state*? Their condition is undoubtedly improved considerably under the Company's government; for the British law has extended its protection to them in common with all, against injury to their lives or limbs, or any great severity of ill usage; but British justice and humanity are not satisfied till they have accomplished all the good that is capable of being done. *The general tranquillity which prevails through the British empire in India, seems to present a favourable opportunity for commencing the work of amelioration, and to withhold it would be to sanction the perpetuity of slavery.*"¶

* Par. Papers on Slavery in India, 1838, p. 315. † p. 318. ‡ p. 356. § 367.

‖ "These different public establishments (the Botanic Gardens at Calcutta) used to be all cultivated by the convicts in chains. In the Botanic Garden their labour is now supplied by peasants hired by the day or week, and the exchange is found cheap, as well as otherwise advantageous; *the labour of freemen here, as elsewhere, being infinitely cheaper than that of slaves.*" (Heber's Journ., vol. 1, p. 43.)

¶ Par. Papers on Slavery in India, 1828, p. 922.

The bearing of the great question of the abolition of slavery in India upon other countries, is vitally important. One of the objects of the British and Foreign Anti-Slavery Society is, "To obtain the unequivocal recognition of the principle, that, *the slave, of whatever clime or colour, entering any portion of the British dominions, shall be free,* the same as upon the shores of the United Kingdom, and to carry this principle into full and complete effect." Who that has considered the state of India, but will sigh, '*O si sic omnia!*' Let Indian slavery be annihilated root and branch; let her indigenous productions be cultivated by an enlightened population, and our common christianity pervade every part of the land, then will "India, emancipated through our instrumentality, from the yoke of a cruel superstition, and admitted to a fellowship in the peace and hopes of the gospel, recognize in Britain, no longer a *conqueror,* to whom she is bound by the terror of our arms, but a benefactor, indissolubly endeared by the triumphs of our mercy." How pungent is the following appeal of that eloquent friend of humanity, G. Thompson, Esq.:—

"There are in North and South America, and on the Islands of the Gulph of Mexico and the Caribean Sea, from *five to six millions* of slaves. To supply the states where the foreign slave trade has not been abolished, a traffic between them and the shores of Africa is carried on, which occasions a loss to that country by sickness, madness, despair, butchery, and slavery, of from three to four hundred thousand per annum. It is put beyond doubt by the calculations in Mr. Buxton's book, that during every revolution of this earth upon its axis, a *thousand human beings are offered in sacrifice, living indeed, upon the reeking shrine of the insatiate Moloch of modern slavery!*—India is the resting place for the lever by which modern Asia is to be raised to more than ancient majesty and glory. Do justice to India, and banish the demon of intestine war from Africa, Do justice to India, and drive the *miscreant manthief* from the banks of the Niger and Gambia. Do justice to India, and see the fetters fall from the limbs of the slave. Do justice to India, and see your wives covered, and your warehouse filled, and your looms busy, and your population clothed with the produce of the East, with the fruits of the industry of the conquered and countless millions who cry from the banks of the Ganges, and the Brahmapootra, and the Indus,—'*If you would redeem Africa, you must regenerate India!*' We must hold public meetings and stir up the mercantile and manufacturing interests; we must memorialize government; we must petition the parliament; we must open the eyes of Abolitionist to this economical mode of effecting the object he seeks. I show you a safe, a peaceful, a profitable, a certain method of abolishing slavery. More hopeful than undertaking to convert the Brazilian or Texian ; less bloody and expensive than the preventative service along the shores of Africa ; and more direct than the influence and success of treaties with insincere nations, or remonstrances with the enlightened but proud and sensative Americans. You need not wait till America is consistent—till Portugal is honest,—you have only to wait till you yourselves are sensible of your power and responsibility ! "

Slavery is justly held in abhorrence in Britain ; and, as the nature and prevalence of this evil in British India are known and lamented, measures will be proposed and urged upon the attention of the legislature for its abolition.* This state of society is inimical to human happiness, and opposed to the improvement and elevation of our species. The author trusts he may adopt the language of the worthy Judge of Bundlecund, whose proposed judicious regulations on the subject of slavery appear to have been disregarded. "I have endeavoured to point out some of the inconveniences of slavery, and aimed at displaying the future advantages of abolishing so inhuman an institution. Aware of the great importance, and convinced of the caution, with which innovation should be attempted, or the ancient laws, customs, or prejudices of a people infringed, I presume not *even to sketch the mode or to fix the period of general emancipation.* Perhaps the sudden manumission of those now actually in a state of bondage, though abstractedly just might be politically unwise. But *there can exist no good reason, either political or humane, against the British government prohibiting the purchase or sale of all slaves, legitimate or illegitimate, after a specified time ; and likewise declaring that all children, male and female, born of parents in a state of slavery, shall from a like date be free.* Should my humble arguments on the subject draw the attention of men possessed of more ability, to investigate and determine the propriety of establishing personal liberty on the

* "In the British Parliament, slavery, and the questions relevant to it, will always be the object of serious discussion. Orators, not less distinguished by the brilliancy of their talent, than by the solidity of their virtue, seconded from without the walls of the senate, by the writings of men gifted with the same qualities, will continue to raise their voice in favour of justice and christian charity. These accents, repeated by the periodical press, will at length resound through each hemisphere, and prove the knell of slavery." Ori. Herald, vol. xiv. p. 96. "On Nobility of Skin."

British model, throughout the Company's provinces, as well as invested with power to extend relief to the objects of my regard, so as to promote a mitigation of their miserable situation, I shall deem myself well rewarded, having no end in view but the honour of my country, and the happiness of my fellow creatures." *

The popular error, that slavery is abolished throughout the British empire, is very mischievous. An amiable, living poet, in an "Ode to the Queen," thus addresses her Majesty:—

> "No slaves within thine empire breathe!
> Before thy steps oppression fly!
> The lamb and lion play beneath
> The meek dominion of thine eye;
> Rule, Victoria, rule the free;
> Chains and fetters yield to thee!"

The importance of correcting this error is self-evident. O may India's cries to British humanity prevail; and may the day speedily dawn, when every subject of the British empire shall be free.

The Rev. Joseph Fenn, late missionary in *Travancore*, in his replies to the questions of the Board of Control relative to slavery in India, very justly observed;—"The slaves are in the lowest possible state of degradation. If it were lawful so to speak of fellow creatures possessing the same capabilities and the same destinies with British christians, I should say they were wild men. *Nothing but christianity descends or can descend low enough to meet them, and to raise them to the level of mankind!* I was a missionary in India, my testimony, therefore, will be received with caution upon this subject. But I am decidedly of opinion, that *the bible is the only book adapted to them in their present state.* If it should please God to allow a free publication of its truths among them, I think it would soon be evident that, independently of the great change it creates in reference to God and eternity, it brings in its train elevation of mind and character, and all the blessings of civilization and education." †—Sep. 1832.

Yes, Britain has a greater boon than civil liberty, to bestow upon her enslaved and superstitious subjects in the East:—

> "——— There is yet a liberty, unsung
> By poets, and by senators unpraised;
> 'Tis liberty of heart, derived from heaven—
> Bought with His blood, who gave it to mankind."—

* Par. Papers on Slavery in India, 1828, p. 303. † 1832, p. 550.

This liberty is revealed in the Gospel of Jesus Christ our Lord. "If the Son shall make you free, ye shall be free indeed." For what purpose is India subjected to Britain, by His fiat who, "ruleth in the kingdom of men, and He appointeth over it whomsoever he will?" Is it not to make his glory known, and hasten the period when it shall be sung in heaven—"The kingdoms of this world are become the kingdoms of our Lord and of his Christ, and he shall reign for ever and ever?" O Britain, my beloved country, consider thy high destiny, and labour, by the messengers of heaven's mercy to man, to make "His way known upon the earth, his saving health among all nations."

"Britain! thy voice can bid the dawn ascend;
On thee alone the eyes of Asia bend.
High Arbitress! to thee her hopes are given
Sole pledge of bliss and delegate of heaven.
In thy dread mantle all her fates repose,
Or bright with blessing, or o'ercast with woes;
And future ages shall thy mandate keep,
Smile at thy touch, or at thy bidding weep.
Oh! to thy godlike destiny arise!
Awake and meet the purpose of the skies!
Wide as thy sceptre waves, let India learn
What virtues round the shrine of empire burn.
Let gentle arts awake at thy behest,
And science soothe the Hindoo's mournful breast.
Be thine the task his drooping eye to cheer,
And elevate his hopes beyond the sphere,
To brighter heavens than proud Sumeeru owns,
Though girt by India and his burning thrones.
Then shall he recognize the beams of day,
And fling at once the fourfold chain away;
Through every limb a sudden life shall start,
And sudden pulses spring around his heart;
Then all their deadened energies shall rise
And vindicate their title to the skies:
Be these thy trophies, Queen of many isles!
Yes, it shall come! E'en now my eyes behold,
In distant view, the wish'd for age unfold;
Lo, o'er the shadowy days that roll between,
A wandering gleam foretels th' ascending scene.
Oh! doom'd victorious from thy wounds to rise,
Dejected India, lift thy downcast eyes,
And mark the hour, whose faithful steps to thee,
Through Time's press'd ranks, brings on the jubilee."*

* Grant's Revival of Learning in the East. 1805.

J HADDON, CASTLE STREET, FINSBURY.